The Low-Carb Air Fryer Cookbook

2000 Days of Savory and Satisfying Dishes to Enhance Your Culinary Journey

Christina J. Williamson

Copyright© 2024 By Christina J. Williamson Rights Reserved

This book is copyright protected. It is only for personal use. You cannot amend, distribute, sell, use, quote or paraphrase any part of the content within this book, without the consent of the author or publisher.

Under no circumstances will any blame or legal responsibility be held against the publisher, or author, for any damages, reparation, or monetary loss due to the information contained within this book, either directly or indirectly.

Limit of Liability/Disclaimer of Warranty:
No book, including this one, can ever replace the diagnostic expertise and medical advice of a physician in providing information about your health. The information contained herein is not intended to replace medical advice. You should consult with your doctor before using the information in this or any health-related book.

The Publisher and the author make no representations or warranties with respect to the accuracy or completeness of the contents of this work and specifically disclaim all warranties, including without limitation warranties of fitness for a particular purpose. No warranty may be created or extended by sales or promotional materials. The advice and strategies contained herein may not be suitable for every situation. This work is sold with the understanding that the Publisher is not engaged in rendering medical, legal, or other professional advice or services. If professional assistance is required, the services of a competent professional person should be sought. Neither the Publisher nor the author shall be liable for damages arising herefrom. The fact that an individual, organization, or website is referred to in this work as a citation and/or potential source of further information does not mean that the author or the Publisher endorses the information the individual, organization, or website may provide or recommendations they/it may make. Further, readers should be aware that websites listed in this work may have changed or disappeared between when this work was written and when it is read.

Manufactured in: USA
Cover Art: DANIELLE REES

Interior Design: DANIELLE REES
Art Producer: BROOKE WHITE

Production Editor: SIENNA ADAMS
Production Manager: SARAH JOHNSON

Editor: AALIYAH LYONS
Photography: MICHAEL SMITH

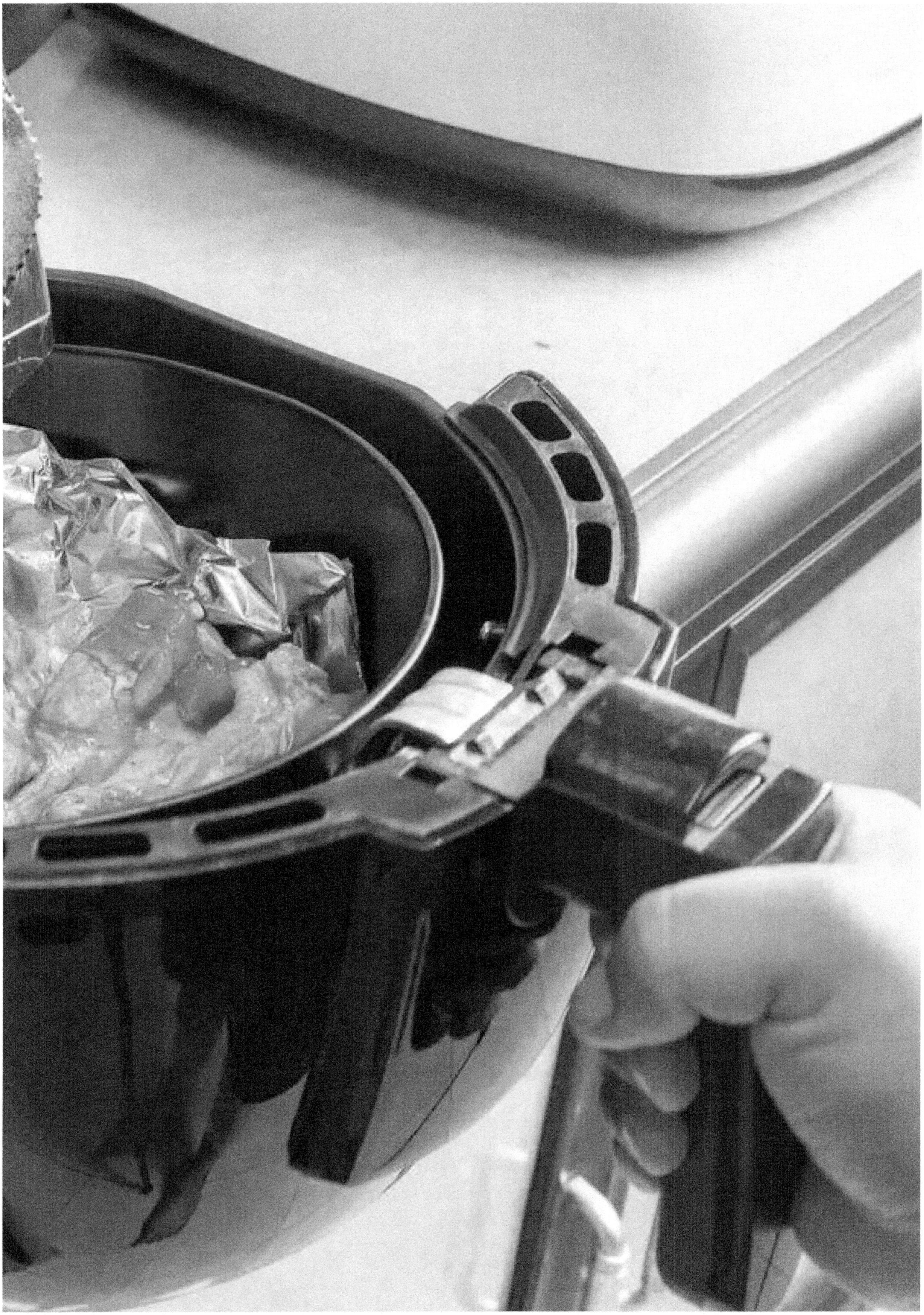

Table Of Contents

Introduction	1	Cheesy Chickpea and Zucchini Burgers	11
		Spinach Balls	11
Chapter 1		Spicy Air-Fried Eggplant	12
Appetizers	7	Crab & Cheese Soufflé	12
French Toasts Cups	8	Spicy Mozzarella Stick	13
Baked Bacon Egg Cups	8	Coconut Pumpkin Curry	13
Keto Wrap	8	Olive, Cheese, and Broccoli	13
Black Beans & Cauliflower Burgers	9	Cream Buns with Strawberries	14
Air-Fried Ratatouille	9	Fried Garlic Green Tomatoes	14
Red Cabbage and Mushroom Stickers	10	Garlic Salmon Balls	14
Vegetable Rolls	10	Fried Zucchini, Squash and Carrot Mix	15
Chickpea & Zucchini Burgers	11	Rice Paper Bacon	15

Sweet & Spicy Tofu with Steamed Spinach	15

Chapter 2
Breakfasts — 16

Creamy Veggie Omelet	17
Coconut Muffins	17
Spiced Baked Eggs	18
Cabbage and Pork Hash	18
Beef and Cabbage Wrap	19
Cinnamon French Toast	19
Mushroom Fritters	20
Seed Porridge	20
Breakfast Chicken Hash	20
Greek Bread	21
Cod Sticks	21
Garlic Bread	22
Cheese Muffins	22
Kale Omelet	22
Chicken Muffins	23
Sausage Bake	23
Tofu Wraps	24
Coriander Sausages Muffins	24
Mozzarella Swirls	24
Chicken and Cream Lasagna	25

Chapter 3
Poultry — 26

Chicken and Arugula Salad	27
Parsley Turkey Stew	27
Chili Chicken Cutlets	27
Pickled Poultry	28
Cream Cheese Chicken	28
Provolone Meatballs	29
Long-Roasted Chicken Thighs	29
Stuffed Turkey	29
Spicy Chicken Roll	30
Oregano Duck Spread	30
Rosemary Chicken Stew	30
Turkey Breast	31
Coated Chicken	31
Buttery Chicken Wings	31
Chicken and Asparagus	32
Sun-dried Tomatoes and Chicken Mix	32
Sweet and Sour Chicken Drumsticks	32
Oregano and Lemon Chicken Drumsticks	33
Asparagus Chicken	33
Chicken with Asparagus and Zucchini	34
Lemon Chicken Mix	34

Chapter 4
Beef, Pork and Lamb — 35

Beef Pie	36
Zucchini Pasta	36
Cheddar Beef Chili	37
Pork Bowls	37
Tender Meat Salad	37
Stuffed Cabbage and Pork Loin Rolls	38
Flavored Pork Chops	38
Dill Pork Shoulder	38
Cilantro Pork Meatballs	39
Air Fryer Pork Satay	39
Stuffed Beef Roll	39
African Style Lamb	40
Lamb Chops with Kalamata Spread	40
Creamy Cheesy Bacon Dip	40
Pork Head Chops with Vegetables	41
Meat Pizza	41
Oregano Pork Chops	41
Beef Under Cabbage Blanket	42
Lamb Fritters	42
Beef Casserole	42
Rosemary Lamb	43
Herbed Pork Skewers	43
Chili Tomato Pork	44
Beef, Lettuce and Cabbage Salad	44
Masala Meatloaf	45
Beef Burger	45

Chapter 5
Fish & Seafood — 46

Shrimp and Spring Onions Stew	47
Crab Dip	47
Tuna Stuffed Avocado	47
Crab Buns	48
Crab Cake	48
Parmesan Garlic Crusted Salmon	49
Sardine Cakes	49

Lime Baked Salmon	50
Ginger Cod Mix	50
Chili Sea Bass Mix	50
Seafood Salad	51
Grilled Salmon with Lemon	51
Stuffed Mackerel	51
Thyme Catfish	52
Cajun Shrimps	52
Squid Stuffed with Cauliflower Mix	52
Lemon and Oregano Tilapia Mix	53
Crispy Fish Sandwiches	53
Air Fryer Shrimp Scampi	53

Chapter 6
Side Dishes and Snacks 54

Eggplant Lasagna	55
Parmesan Cauliflower Risotto	55
Mushroom Cakes	56
Pork Minis	56
Air Fryer Buffalo Cauliflower	56
Parm Squash	57
Seafood Balls	57
Pull-apart Bread with Garlic Oil	57
Portobello Patties	58
Cauliflower Bites	58
Keto Granola	58
Potato Filled Bread Rolls	59
Kale & Celery Crackers	59
Spinach Mash	59
Cream Cheese Zucchini	60
Almond Brussels Sprouts	60
Fried Broccoli From India	60
Sweet Potato Cauliflower Patties	61
Almond Broccoli Rice	61

Chapter 7
Vegan & Vegetarian 62

Veggie Pizza	63
Mediterranean Vegetable Skewers	63
Smoked Tempeh	63
Fried Pickles	64
Eggplant Dip	64
Vegetarian Hash Browns	65
Feta & Mushroom Frittata	65

Sweet Potato Fritters	66
Okra Salad	66
Cheesy Rutabaga	66
Mustard Cabbage	67
Mushroom, Onion and Feta Frittata	67
Greens Salad	67
Buffalo Cauliflower Wings	68
Spicy Glazed Carrots	68
Spinach Tortillas	68
Cheese Stuffed Mushrooms	69
Cauliflower Balls	69
Cauliflower Pizza Crust	69
Cream Cheese Green Beans	70
Feta Peppers	70
Herbed Asparagus and Sauce	71
Mixed Veggies	71

Chapter 8
Desserts 72

Chia and Hemp Pudding	73
Artichokes and Cream Cheese Dip	73
Creamy Cheddar Eggs	73
Baked Apple	74
Date & Hazelnut Cookies	74
Cheddar Biscuits	74
Lemon Olives Dip	75
Mint Cake	75
Lemon Pie	75
Toffee Apple Upside-Down Breakfast Cake	76
Crustless Cheesecake	76
Turmeric Chicken Cubes	77
Cheese Pies	77
Coconut Cheese Sticks	78
Olives Fritters	78
Herbed Cheese Balls	78

Appendix 1 Measurement Conversion Chart	79
Appendix 2 The Dirty Dozen and Clean Fifteen	80
Appendix 3 Index	81

Introduction

In a world where dietary trends come and go like fleeting fads, there's one that has consistently stood the test of time and science: the low-carb diet. This dietary approach has not only gained immense popularity but has also proven its efficacy in achieving various health and wellness goals. If you've found yourself on this culinary journey, you are about to embark on a path that can transform your life. The Low-Carb Air Fryer Cookbook is here to guide you on this exciting adventure, offering a wealth of delicious low-carb recipes that you can prepare with the modern kitchen marvel known as the air fryer.

Understanding the Low-Carb Diet

WHAT IS A LOW-CARB DIET?

A low-carb diet, as the name suggests, is centered around the reduction of carbohydrates in your daily meals. Carbohydrates are a primary source of energy, but when consumed in excess, they can lead to weight gain and various health issues. By lowering your carb intake and replacing those calories with healthy fats and proteins, you can reprogram your body to burn fat for fuel. This metabolic shift can lead to weight loss, improved blood sugar control, and a host of other health benefits.

THE BENEFITS OF A LOW-CARB DIET

The advantages of a low-carb diet are numerous and far-reaching. This dietary approach has been associated with:

- Weight Loss: By reducing carb intake, you can control your appetite and achieve a calorie deficit, making it easier to shed those extra pounds.
- Improved Blood Sugar Control: Low-carb diets can be an effective tool in managing type 2 diabetes and stabilizing blood sugar levels.
- Enhanced Heart Health: Lowering carbohydrate intake can lead to improvements in heart health by reducing risk factors like high blood pressure and triglyceride levels.
- Mental Clarity: Some individuals report improved mental clarity and focus when following a low-carb diet.
- Increased Energy: As your body adapts to burning fat for fuel, you may experience more sustained energy throughout the day.

Exploring the World of Air Frying

HOW DOES AN AIR FRYER WORK?

Air fryers use convection heating to circulate hot air around the food, providing that coveted crispy texture. By using a minimal amount of oil or even none at all, you can transform high-carb, deep-fried favorites into low-carb, guilt-free delights.

EFFICIENCY AND CONVENIENCE

The air fryer is a game-changer in the kitchen. Its speed, convenience, and versatility make it a valuable addition to any low-carb cooking arsenal. You can whip up a variety of dishes *quickly and efficiently without sacrificing flavor or health benefits. Whether you're a seasoned chef or a kitchen novice, the air fryer simplifies the cooking process, making it accessible to all.*

A HEALTHIER WAY TO ENJOY "FRIED" FOODS

The air fryer's ability to crisp up food with minimal oil is a culinary innovation. Traditional deep frying can load your meals with unhealthy fats and unnecessary calories. The air fryer, on the other hand, allows you to achieve that desired crispy texture with minimal oil, making it the perfect choice for anyone on a low-carb diet.

Achieving Low-Carb Success with an Air Fryer

Now that you understand the principles of a low-carb diet, let's explore how the air fryer can be your secret weapon in this culinary journey. The air fryer is not just another kitchen gadget; it's a versatile appliance that allows you to enjoy the delicious crunch and flavor of fried food without the excessive use of oil and carbohydrates.

THE AIR FRYER'S ROLE IN LOW-CARB COOKING

Incorporating an air fryer into your low-carb lifestyle offers numerous benefits:

- Reduced Oil Intake: Say goodbye to deep frying and the unnecessary calories and unhealthy fats that come with it. Air frying uses significantly less oil, making it a perfect fit for a low-carb diet.
- Faster Cooking: Air fryers cook food faster than traditional ovens, making it a convenient choice for busy individuals.
- Crispy Texture: Enjoy the satisfying crunch of your favorite dishes without the carb overload.
- Versatility: Air fryers can handle a wide variety of low-carb ingredients, from vegetables and proteins to low-carb breading alternatives.

Using This Cookbook

As you delve into The Low-Carb Air Fryer Cookbook, you'll find a treasure trove of recipes that cater to various tastes and dietary preferences. But to make the most of this culinary guide, it's important to know how to navigate its pages effectively.

RECIPE CATEGORIES

This cookbook is divided into sections that cover a wide range of low-carb dishes, including:

- Breakfast Delights: Start your day with delicious low-carb breakfast options.
- Appetizers and Snacks: Satisfy your cravings with crispy and flavorful bites.
- Main Courses: Discover an array of low-carb main dishes, from chicken and fish to vegetarian delights.
- Sides and Vegetables: Elevate your meal with creative and low-carb side dishes.
- Desserts: Indulge your sweet tooth with low-carb treats that won't derail your diet.

RECIPE FEATURES

Each recipe in this book is designed to be:

- Low-Carb: All recipes are carefully crafted to be low in carbohydrates, allowing you to maintain your dietary goals.
- Delicious: Taste is paramount, and these recipes have been developed with flavor in mind.
- Air Fryer-Friendly: Clear instructions guide you on how to use your air fryer effectively for each recipe.
- Nutritional Information: Nutritional facts for each dish are provided, helping you track your carb intake with ease.

GETTING STARTED

To get the most out of this cookbook, we recommend that you:

- Read the introduction for essential tips on air frying and low-carb cooking.
- Familiarize yourself with the air fryer settings and functions.
- Plan your meals ahead and create a shopping list of low-carb ingredients.
- Experiment and enjoy the process. The world of low-carb cooking is a journey of discovery, so don't be afraid to get creative!

The Low-Carb Air Fryer Cookbook is more than just a collection of recipes; it's your guide to a healthier and more satisfying way of eating. We hope this cookbook will inspire you to embrace the low-carb lifestyle, armed with the incredible potential of the air fryer to create scrumptious, low-carb meals that will leave your taste buds dancing and your health thriving.

Get ready to embark on a culinary adventure that's as rewarding as it is delicious. Happy cooking!

Air Fryer Cooking Chart

Beef					
Item	Temp (°F)	Time (mins)	Item	Temp (°F)	Time (mins)
Beef Eye Round Roast (4 lbs.)	400 °F	45 to 55	Meatballs (1-inch)	370 °F	7
Burger Patty (4 oz.)	370 °F	16 to 20	Meatballs (3-inch)	380 °F	10
Filet Mignon (8 oz.)	400 °F	18	Ribeye, bone-in (1-inch, 8 oz)	400 °F	10 to 15
Flank Steak (1.5 lbs.)	400 °F	12	Sirloin steaks (1-inch, 12 oz)	400 °F	9 to 14
Flank Steak (2 lbs.)	400 °F	20 to 28			

Chicken					
Item	Temp (°F)	Time (mins)	Item	Temp (°F)	Time (mins)
Breasts, bone in (1 1/4 lb.)	370 °F	25	Legs, bone-in lb.)	380 °F	30
Breasts, boneless (4 oz)	380 °F	12	Thighs, boneless (1 1/2 lb.)	380 °F	18 to 20
Drumsticks (2 1/2 lb.)	370 °F	20	Wings (2 lb.)	400 °F	12
Game Hen (halved 2 lb.)	390 °F	20	Whole Chicken	360 °F	75
Thighs, bone-in (2 lb.)	380 °F	22	Tenders	360 °F	8 to 10

Pork & Lamb						
Item	Temp (°F)	Time (mins)	Item	Temp (°F)	Time (mins)
Bacon (regular)	400 °F	5 to 7	Pork Tenderloin	370 °F	15
Bacon (thick cut)	400 °F	6 to 10	Sausages	380 °F	15
Pork Loin (2 lb.)	360 °F	55	Lamb Loin Chops (1-inch thick)	400 °F	8 to 12
Pork Chops, bone in (1-inch, 6.5 oz)	400 °F	12	Rack of Lamb (1.5 - lb.)	380 °F	22
Flank Steak (2 lbs.)	400 °F	20 to 28			

Fish & Seafood						
Item	Temp (°F)	Time (mins)	Item	Temp (°F)	Time (mins)
Calamari (8 oz)	400 °F	4	Tuna Steak	400 °F	7 to 10
Fish Fillet (1-inch, 8 oz)	400 °F	10	Scallops	400 °F	5 to 7
Salmon, fillet (6 oz)	380 °F	12	Shrimp	400 °F	5
Swordfish steak	400 °F	10	Sirloin steaks (1-inch, 12 oz)	400 °F	9 to 14
Flank Steak (2 lbs.)	400 °F	20 to 28			

Vegetables					
INGREDIENT	**AMOUNT**	**PREPARATION**	**OIL**	**TEMP**	**COOK TIME**
Asparagus	2 bunches	Cut in half, trim stems	2 Tbsp	420°F	12-15 mins
Beets	1 1/2 lbs	Peel, cut in 1/2-inch cubes	1 Tbsp	390°F	28-30 mins
Bell peppers (for roasting)	4 peppers	Cut in quarters, remove seeds	1 Tbsp	400°F	15-20 mins
Broccoli	1 large head	Cut in 1-2-inch florets	1 Tbsp	400°F	15-20 mins
Brussels sprouts	1 lb	Cut in half, remove stems	1 Tbsp	425°F	15-20 mins
Carrots	1 lb	Peel, cut in 1/4-inch rounds	1 Tbsp	425°F	10-15 mins
Cauliflower	1 head	Cut in 1-2-inch florets	2 Tbsp	400°F	20-22 mins
Corn on the cob	7 ears	Whole ears, remove husks	1 Tbps	400°F	14-17 mins
Green beans	1 bag (12 oz)	Trim	1 Tbps	420°F	18-20 mins
Kale (for chips)	4 OZ	Tear into pieces, remove stems	None	325°F	5-8 mins
Mushrooms	16 OZ	Rinse, slice thinly	1 Tbps	390°F	25-30 mins
Potatoes, russet	1 1/2 lbs	Cut in 1-inch wedges	1 Tbps	390°F	25-30 mins
Potatoes, russet	1 lb	Hand-cut fries, soak 30 mins in cold water, then pat dry	1/2 -3 Tbps	400°F	25-28 mins
Potatoes, sweet	1 lb	Hand-cut fries, soak 30 mins in cold water, then pat dry	1 Tbps	400°F	25-28 mins
Zucchini	1 lb	Cut in eighths lengthwise, then cut in half	1 Tbps	400°F	15-20 mins

Chapter 1

Appetizers

French Toasts Cups

Prep time: 12 minutes | Cook time: 9 minutes | Serves 2

- 1/3 cup coconut flour
- 1 egg, beaten
- ¼ teaspoon baking powder
- 2 teaspoons Erythritol
- ¼ teaspoon ground cinnamon
- 1 teaspoon mascarpone
- 1 tablespoon butter, softened

1. In the mixing bowl, mix coconut flour with egg, baking powder, Erythritol, ground cinnamon, and mascarpone.
2. Then grease the baking cups with butter and pour the coconut flour mixture inside.
3. Bake the meal at 365°F for 9 minutes or until the mixture is set.

PER SERVING

Calories: 168 | Fat: 10.3g | Fiber: 8.2g | Carbs: 14.1g | Protein: 5.8 g

Baked Bacon Egg Cups

Prep time: 10 minutes | Cook time: 8 minutes | Serves 4

- 2 eggs
- 1 tablespoon chives, fresh, chopped
- ½ teaspoon paprika
- ½ teaspoon cayenne pepper
- 3-ounces cheddar cheese, shredded
- ½ teaspoon butter
- ¼ teaspoon salt
- 4-ounces bacon, cut into tiny pieces

1. Slice bacon into tiny pieces and sprinkle it with cayenne pepper, salt, and paprika. Mix the chopped bacon. Spread butter in bottom of ramekin dishes and beat the eggs there. Add the chives and shredded cheese. Add the chopped bacon over egg mixture in ramekin dishes.
2. Place the ramekins in your air fryer basket. Preheat your air fryer to 360°F.
3. When the cook time is completed, remove the ramekins from air fryer and serve warm.

PER SERVING

Calories: 553 | Total Fat: 43.3g | Carbs: 2.3g | Protein: 37.3g

Keto Wrap

Prep time: 10 minutes | Cook time: 15 minutes | Serves 2

- ½ cup ground pork
- 1 jalapeno pepper, chopped
- 1 teaspoon coconut oil
- 1 teaspoon plain yogurt
- ½ teaspoon dried oregano
- 4 lettuce leaves

1. Mix the ground pork with jalapeno pepper and ground oregano.
2. Then preheat the air fryer to 365°F.
3. Then fill lettuce leaves with ground pork mixture. Add plain yogurt and wrap the lettuce leaves.

PER SERVING

Calories: 141 | Fat: 10.4g | Fiber: 0.4g | Carbs: 1.1g | Protein: 10.3

The Low-Carb Air Fryer Cookbook

Black Beans & Cauliflower Burgers

Prep time: 10 minutes | Cook time: 15 minutes | Serves 4

- 3 cloves garlic, minced
- 1 tablespoon basil leaves, minced
- 1 teaspoon olive oil
- 1 teaspoon chili sauce
- 1 tablespoon vegan oyster sauce
- ¾ cup vegan mayonnaise
- 4 large tomatoes, sliced
- 2 tablespoons potato starch
- 1 tablespoon flaxseed mixed with 3 tablespoons water
- 1 cup black beans
- 1 large head cauliflower, cut into florets
- 1 tablespoon rice vinegar
- 1 large avocado, mashed

1. Prepare all ingredients by washing all the veggies. Cut the cauliflower, then soak it in a pot of warm water for a couple of minutes. Soak black beans in a pot of warm water with cauliflower. Rinse them with cold water, then pat dry. Check they are dry before you put them into a food processor.
2. Add vegan oyster sauce, rice vinegar, chili sauce, and olive oil into food processor and season with salt and pepper. Add basil leaves and garlic. Now, blend until the mixture becomes rice-like in its consistency. Transfer the mixture to a bowl and set aside. Clean the food processor, then add flax seed and 3 tablespoons of water and blend mixture until it becomes fluffy. Transfer this mixture to the bowl with cauliflower mixture, add potato starch and toss to blend ingredients.
3. Shape burger mixture into big balls and flatten on a baking sheet to make burger patties. Now, preheat your air fryer to 360°F for 2-minutes. Now place enough burger patties in the air-fryer basket. Cook for 15-minutes. Make sure to flip the patties halfway through the cook time. Prepare the tomatoes and cut avocado into halves and remove the pit. Scoop the avocado flesh and mash in a bowl with a fork. Use the veggie burgers as buns.
4. Start with one veggie burger at bottom, followed by mashed avocado, then a slice of tomato. Spread some vegan mayonnaise on top of tomato and cover with another veggie burger. Serve warm.

PER SERVING

Calories: 124 | Total Fat: 4.41g | Carbs: 9.99g | Protein: 10.99g

Air-Fried Ratatouille

Prep time: 10 minutes | Cook time: 15 minutes | Serves 4

- 1 onion, peeled, cubed
- 1 clove garlic, crushed
- 1 tablespoon olive oil
- 2 tomatoes, chopped
- fresh ground pepper
- 2 teaspoons provencal herbs
- 1 large zucchini, sliced
- 1 yellow bell pepper, chopped

1. Preheat your air-fryer to 300°F. In an oven-proof bowl, add vegetables, salt, pepper and olive oil and mix well. Put the bowl in the basket in air fryer.
2. Cook for 15-minutes, stirring halfway through cook time. Serve with fricasseed meat.

PER SERVING

Calories: 154 | Total Fat: 12.05g | Carbs: 11.94g | Protein: 1.69g

Red Cabbage and Mushroom Stickers

Prep time: 12 minutes | Cook time: 15 minutes | Serves 4

- 1 cup red cabbage, shredded
- 1/4 cup button mushrooms, chopped
- 1/4 cup carrot, grated
- 2 tbsp. onion, minced
- 2 garlic cloves, minced
- 2 tsp. fresh ginger, grated
- 12 Gyoza potsticker wrappers
- 2 1/2 tsp. olive oil, divided
- 1 tbsp. water

1. Combine the red cabbage, mushrooms, carrot, onion, garlic, and ginger in a baking pan. Add 1 tbsp. of water. Place in the air fryer and bake at 370°F for 6 minutes, until the vegetables are crisp-tender. Drain and set aside.
2. Working one at a time, place the potsticker wrappers on a work surface. Top each wrapper with a scant 1 tbsp. of the filling. Fold half of the wrapper over the other half to form a half-circle. Dab with water and press both edges together.
3. Spread 1 1/4 tsp. of olive oil on the baking pan. Put half of the potstickers, seam-side up, in the pan. Air fry for 5 minutes. Add 1 tbsp. of water and return the pan to the air fryer.
4. Air fry for 4 minutes more, or until hot. Repeat with the remaining potstickers, the remaining 1 1/4 tsp. of oil, and another tbsp. of water. Serve immediately.

PER SERVING

Calories: 87.5 | Fat: 2.8g | Protein: 2.5g | Carbs: 13.5g | Fiber: 1g, Sugar: 1g

Vegetable Rolls

Prep time: 10 minutes | Cook time: 8 minutes | Serves 4

- toasted sesame seeds
- 2 carrots, grated
- spring roll wrappers
- 1 egg white
- a dash gluten-free soy sauce
- ½ cabbage, sliced
- 2 tbsp. olive oil

1. In a pan over high flame heat, 2 tbsp. of oil and sauté the chopped vegetables. Add soy sauce, turn off the heat, and add toasted sesame seeds. Lay rolls on a surface and spread egg white with a brush.
2. Add some vegetable mix in the wrapper and fold.
3. Spray the rolls with oil spray and cook in the Air Fryer for 8 minutes at 380°F.

PER SERVING

Calories: 125.4 | Protein: 12.4g | Carbs: 7.6g | Fat: 14.6g

Chickpea & Zucchini Burgers

Prep time: 10 minutes | Cook time: 10 minutes | Serves 4

- 1 can of chickpeas, strained
- 1 red onion, diced
- 2 eggs, beaten
- 1-ounce almond flour
- 3 tablespoons coriander
- 1 teaspoon garlic puree
- 1-ounce cheddar cheese, shredded
- 1 courgette, spiralized
- 1 teaspoon chili powder
- salt and pepper to taste
- 1 teaspoon mixed spice

1. Add your ingredients to a bowl and mix well. Shape portions of the mixture into burgers.
2. Place in the air fryer for 15-minutes until cooked.

PER SERVING

Calories: 263 | Total Fat: 11.2g | Carbs: 8.3g | Protein: 6.3g

Cheesy Chickpea and Zucchini Burgers

Prep time: 7 minutes | Cook time: 15 minutes | Serves 4

- 1 can chickpeas, drained
- 3 tbsp. coriander
- 1 oz. cheddar cheese, shredded
- 2 eggs, beaten
- 1 tsp. garlic puree
- 1 zucchini spiralized
- 1 red onion, diced
- 1 tsp. chili powder
- 1 tsp. mixed spice
- Salt and pepper to taste
- 1 tsp. cumin

1. Mix all the ingredients in a mixing bowl.
2. Shape portions of the mixture into burgers. Place in the air fryer at 300°F for 15 minutes.

PER SERVING

Calories: 184.1 | Fat: 9.7g | Carbs: 18.1g | Protein: 12.8g

Spinach Balls

Prep time: 10 minutes | Cook time: 20 minutes | Serves 4

- 1 carrot, peeled and grated
- 1 tablespoon corn flour
- 1 tablespoon nutritional yeast
- 1 egg, beaten
- ½ teaspoon garlic powder
- ½ onion, chopped
- 1 package fresh spinach, blanched and chopped

1. Blend ingredients in a bowl, except the breadcrumbs. Make small balls with mixture and roll them over the bread crumbs.
2. Place the spinach balls in your air fryer at 390°F for a cook time of 10-minutes. Serve warm.

PER SERVING

Calories: 262 | Total Fat: 11.2g | Carbs: 7.4g | Protein: 7.8g

Spicy Air-Fried Eggplant

Prep time: 10 minutes | Cook time: 20 minutes | Serves 4

- 2 garlic cloves, minced
- 2 large eggplants, sliced
- 2 red chili peppers, chopped
- 2 green chili peppers, minced
- 1 teaspoon sesame oil
- 1 tablespoon light soy sauce
- pepper and salt to taste

1. Cut eggplants and set aside. Chop chilies and mince garlic and save for later use. In a bowl, mix garlic, green and red chili peppers. Add soy sauce and sprinkle with pepper, add eggplant slices, toss and set aside.
2. Preheat your air-fryer to 350°F. Add eggplant slices and spray with sesame oil. Cook for 20-minutes, shake basket every 5-minutes during cook time. Once cooked garnish eggplant slices with chili peppers and garlic. Serve warm.

PER SERVING

Calories: 223 | Total Fat: 6.4g | Carbs: 11.8g | Protein: 3.2g

Crab & Cheese Soufflé

Prep time: 10 minutes | Cook time: 18 minutes | Serves 2

- 1 lb. cooked crab meat
- 1 capsicum
- 1 small onion, diced
- 1 cup cream
- 1 cup milk
- 4-ounces brie
- brandy to cover crab meat
- 3 eggs
- 5 drops liquid stevia
- 3-ounces cheddar cheese, grated
- 4 cups bread, cubed

1. Soak the cram meat in brandy and 4-parts water. Loosen the meat in brandy. Sauté onion and bread. Grate cheddar cheese and mix ingredients. In the same pan, add some of the butter and stir for a minute. Add the crab to pan. Add ½ of the milk and 1 tablespoon of brandy and cook for 2-minutes.
2. Add the bread cubes to frying pan and mix well. Sprinkle with cheese and pepper. Put the stuffing in 5 ramekins, without brushing them with oil. Distribute the brie evenly. In a bowl, combine ½ cup of cream with stevia. Heat the cream in a pan and add remaining milk. Pour mixture into ramekins. Preheat your air fryer to 350°Fahreneheit add dish and cook for 20-minutes.

PER SERVING

Calories: 202 | Total Fat: 5.6g | Carbs: 6.2g | Protein: 14.3g

Spicy Mozzarella Stick

Prep time: 10 minutes | Cook time: 5 minutes | Serves 3

- 8-ounces mozzarella cheese, cut into strips
- 2 tablespoons olive oil
- ½ teaspoon salt
- 1 cup pork rinds
- 1 egg
- 1 teaspoon garlic powder
- 1 teaspoon paprika

1. Cut the mozzarella into 6 strips. Whisk the egg along with salt, paprika, and garlic powder. Dip the mozzarella strips into egg mixture first, then into pork rinds. Arrange them on a baking platter and place in the fridge for 30-minutes.
2. Preheat your air fryer to 360°F. Drizzle olive oil into the air fryer. Arrange the mozzarella sticks in the air fryer and cook for about 5-minutes. Make sure to turn them at least twice, to ensure they will become golden on all sides.

PER SERVING

Calories: 156 | Total Fat: 9.6g | Carbs: 1.89g | Protein: 16g

Coconut Pumpkin Curry

Prep time: 10 minutes | Cook time: 25 minutes | Serves 4

- 2 cups pumpkin, cubed
- 1 tablespoon sesame seeds
- 2-inches ginger, minced
- 1 tablespoon parsley, chopped
- 2 teaspoons curry powder
- 1 teaspoon black pepper
- ¼ cup coconut cream
- 1 tablespoon shredded coconut
- 1 red chili for garnish
- 1 red chili, minced
- ¼ cup water

1. Place the cubed pumpkin into the pan with minced ginger. Add ¼ cup water and ¼ cup coconut cream into the pan. Cook for 15-minutes at 300°F. Slightly mash pumpkin cubes.
2. Add the minced chili, curry powder, pepper, and stir. Cook for another 10-minutes. Transfer to a large bowl. Garnish with chopped parsley and red chili. Serve warm.

PER SERVING

Calories: 115 | Total Fat: 4.38g | Carbs: 19.85 | Protein: 2.7g

Olive, Cheese, and Broccoli

Prep time: 7 minutes | Cook time: 15 minutes | Serves 4

- 2 lbs. broccoli florets
- 2 tbsp. olive oil
- 1/4 cup Parmesan cheese shaved
- 2 tsp. lemon zest, grated
- 1/3 cup Kalamata olives (halved, pitted
- 1/2 tsp. ground black pepper
- 1 tsp. sea salt
- Water

1. Boil the water in a pan over medium heat and cook the broccoli for about 4 minutes. Drain. Add the broccoli with salt, pepper, and olive oil in a bowl.
2. Place in the air fryer and cook at 400°F for 15 minutes.
3. Stir twice during the Cooking Time. Place on a plate and toss with lemon zest, cheese, and olives.

PER SERVING

Calories: 213.5 | Fat: 13.2g | Carbs: 12.8g | Protein: 12.9g

Cream Buns with Strawberries

Prep time: 10 minutes | Cook time: 12 minutes | Serves 6

- 240g all-purpose flour
- 50g granulated sugar
- 8g baking powder
- 1g of salt
- 85g chopped cold butter
- 2 large eggs
- 10 ml vanilla extract
- 5 ml of water

1. Sift flour, sugar, baking powder and salt in a large bowl. Put the butter with the flour with the use of a blender or your hands until the mixture resembles thick crumbs.
2. Mix the strawberries in the flour mixture 1 egg and the vanilla extract in a separate bowl.
3. Put the cream mixture in the flour mixture until they are homogeneous, and then spread the mixture to a thickness of 38 mm.
4. Use a round cookie cutter to cut the buns. Spread the buns with a combination of egg and water. Set aside
5. Preheat the air fryer, set it to 375°F.
6. Place baking paper in the preheated inner basket. Place the buns on top and cook for 12 minutes.

PER SERVING

Calories: 149 | Fat: 13.4g | Carbs: 2.8g | Protein: 11.2g, Sugar: 7.6g

Fried Garlic Green Tomatoes

Prep time: 10 minutes | Cook time: 12 minutes | Serves 2

- 3 green tomatoes, sliced
- ½ cup almond flour
- 2 eggs, beaten
- salt and pepper to taste
- 1 teaspoon garlic, minced

1. Season the tomatoes with salt, garlic and pepper. Preheat your air fryer to 400°F. Dip the tomatoes first in flour then in egg mixture.
2. Spray the tomato rounds with olive oil and place in air fryer basket. Cook for 8-minutes, then flip over and cook for an additional 4-minutes. Serve with zero carb mayonnaise.

PER SERVING

Calories: 123 | Total Fat: 3.9g | Carbs: 16g | Protein: 8.4g

Garlic Salmon Balls

Prep time: 10 minutes | Cook time: 15 minutes | Serves 2

- 6-ounces of tinned salmon
- 1 large egg
- 3 tablespoons olive oil
- 5 tablespoons wheat germ
- ½ teaspoon garlic powder
- 1 tablespoon dill, fresh, chopped
- 4 tablespoons spring onion, diced
- 4 tablespoons celery, diced

1. Preheat your air fryer to 370°F. In a large bowl, mix the salmon, the egg, celery, onion, dill, and garlic.
2. Shape the mixture into golf ball size balls and roll them in the wheat germ. In a small pan, warm olive oil over medium-low heat. Add the salmon balls and slowly flatten them. Transfer them to your air fryer and cook for 10-minutes.

PER SERVING

Calories: 219 | Total Fat: 7.7g | Carbs: 14.8g | Protein: 23.1g

Fried Zucchini, Squash and Carrot Mix

Prep time: 10 minutes | Cook time: 35 minutes | Serves 4

- ½ lb. carrots, peeled and cubed
- 6 teaspoons olive oil
- 1 lb. zucchini, chopped into half-moons
- 1 lb. yellow squash, chopped in half-moons
- 1 teaspoon sea salt
- ½ teaspoon white pepper
- 1 tablespoon tarragon leaves, chopped

1. Toss carrots in a bowl with 2 teaspoons of olive oil, then place them into air fryer basket. Cook for 5-minutes at 400°F.
2. Toss the zucchini and squash in the rest of the oil, salt and pepper and place into air fryer. Cook for 30-minutes, tossing three times during cook time. Toss with tarragon and serve.

PER SERVING

Calories: 217 | Total Fat: 4.2g | Carbs: 3.9g | Protein: 6.2g

Rice Paper Bacon

Prep time: 10 minutes | Cook time: 30 minutes | Serves 4

- 4 pieces white rice paper,
- cut into 1-inch thick strips
- 2 tablespoons water
- 2 tablespoons liquid smoke
- 2 tablespoons cashew butter
- 3 tablespoons soy sauce or tamari

1. Preheat your air fryer to 350°F. In a mixing bowl, add soy sauce, cashew butter, liquid smoke, and water, mix well. Soak the rice paper in this mixture for 5 minutes.
2. Place the rice paper in air fryer and do not overlap pieces. Air fry for 15-minutes or until crispy. Serve with steamed vegetables!

PER SERVING

Calories: 232 | Total Fat: 7.4g | Carbs: 6.2g | Protein: 7.3g

Sweet & Spicy Tofu with Steamed Spinach

Prep time: 10 minutes | Cook time: 24 minutes | Serves 6

- 6 cups of spinach, chopped
- 2 teaspoons rice vinegar
- 1 teaspoon agave syrup
- 1 teaspoon salt
- 2-inches ginger, minced
- 1 teaspoon sesame oil
- 1 tablespoon vegan oyster sauce
- 1 teaspoon red pepper flakes
- 1 lb. tofu cubed

1. Rinse and drain the tofu. Make sure to press the tofu to remove excess water. Cut tofu into small cubes and place them in a mixing bowl. Add minced ginger to bowl with tofu. Add agave syrup, season with salt, red pepper flakes and stir. Let mixture stand for 30-minutes before frying.
2. Prepare spinach by steaming for 4-minutes, then transfer spinach to bowl. Add vegan oyster sauce and rice vinegar and toss and save for later use. Preheat air-fryer to 370°F. Once cooked, transfer the tofu to bowl with steamed spinach mix. Toss all ingredients and serve warm.

PER SERVING

Calories: 169 | Total Fat: 10.8g | Carbs: 6.8g | Protein: 15.2g

Chapter 2

Breakfasts

Creamy Veggie Omelet

Prep time: 10 minutes | **Cook time:** 14 minutes | **Serves 4**

- 4 eggs, beaten
- 1 tablespoon cream cheese
- ½ teaspoon chili flakes
- ½ cup broccoli florets, chopped
- ¼ teaspoon salt
- ¼ cup heavy cream
- ¼ teaspoon white pepper
- Cooking spray

1. Put the beaten eggs in the big bowl.
2. Add chili flakes, salt, and white pepper.
3. with the help of the hand whisker stir the liquid until the salt is dissolved.
4. Then add cream cheese and heavy cream.
5. Stir the ingredients until you get the homogenous liquid.
6. After this, add broccoli florets.
7. Preheat the air fryer to 375°F.
8. Spray the air fryer basket with cooking spray from inside.
9. Pour the egg liquid in the air fryer basket.
10. Cook the omelet for 14 minutes.

PER SERVING

Calories: 102| Fat: 8.1| Fiber: 0.3| Carbs: 1.5| Protein: 6.2

Coconut Muffins

Prep time: 10 minutes | **Cook time:** 10 minutes | **Serves 2**

- 1/3 cup almond flour
- 2 tablespoons Erythritol
- ¼ teaspoon baking powder
- 1 teaspoon apple cider vinegar
- 1 tablespoon coconut milk
- 1 tablespoon coconut oil, softened
- 1 teaspoon ground cinnamon
- Cooking spray

1. In the mixing bowl mix up almond flour.
2. Erythritol, baking powder, and ground cinnamon.
3. Add apple cider vinegar, coconut milk, and coconut oil.
4. Stir the mixture until smooth.
5. Spray the muffin molds with cooking spray.
6. Scoop the muffin batter in the muffin molds.
7. Spray the surface of every muffin with the help of the spatula.
8. Preheat the air fryer to 365°F.
9. Insert the rack in the air fryer.
10. Place the muffins on the rack and cook them for 10 minutes at 365°F.
11. Then cool the cooked muffins well and remove them from the molds.

PER SERVING

Calories: 107| Fat: 10.9| Fiber: 1.3| Carbs: 2.7| Protein: 1.2

Spiced Baked Eggs

Prep time:10 minutes |Cook time: 3 minutes |Serves 2

- 2 eggs
- 1 teaspoon mascarpone
- ¼ teaspoon ground nutmeg
- ¼ teaspoon dried basil
- ¼ teaspoon dried oregano
- ¼ teaspoon dried cilantro
- ¼ teaspoon ground turmeric
- ¼ teaspoon onion powder
- ¼ teaspoon salt

1. Crack the eggs in the mixing bowl and whisk them well.
2. After this, add mascarpone and stir until you get a homogenous mixture.
3. Then add all spices and mix up the liquid gently.
4. Pour it in the silicone egg molds and transfer in the air fryer basket.
5. Cook the egg cups for 3 minutes at 400F.

PER SERVING

Calories: 72| Fat: 4.9| Fiber: 0.2| Carbs: 1.1| Protein: 5.9

Cabbage and Pork Hash

Prep time:15 minutes |Cook time: 20 minutes |Serves 4

- 1 Chinese cabbage, shredded
- ¼ cup chicken broth
- ½ teaspoon keto tomato sauce
- 1 green bell pepper, chopped
- 1 teaspoon salt
- 6 oz pork loin, chopped
- 1 tablespoon apple cider vinegar
- 1 teaspoon sesame oil
- ½ teaspoon chili flakes
- ½ teaspoon salt
- ¼ teaspoon ground black pepper
- 1 teaspoon ground turmeric

1. Put Chinese cabbage in the bowl.
2. Add chicken broth, tomato sauce, bell pepper, and salt.
3. Mix up the ingredients and transfer in the air fryer basket.
4. Cook the cabbage for 5 minutes at 365°F.
5. Meanwhile, in the mixing bowl mix up ground black pepper, turmeric, salt, chili flakes, sesame oil, and apple cider vinegar.
6. Add chopped pork loin and mix up the ingredients.
7. Add the meat in the air fryer and cook the cabbage hash for 10 minutes at 385F.
8. Then shake the hash well and cook it for 5 minutes more.

PER SERVING

Calories: 131| Fat: 7.3| Fiber: 0.8| Carbs: 3.3| Protein: 12.6

The Low-Carb Air Fryer Cookbook | **18**

Beef and Cabbage Wrap

Prep time: 10 minutes | Cook time: 15 minutes | Serves 2

- ½ cup ground beef
- ½ jalapeno pepper, chopped
- ¼ teaspoon ground black pepper
- ½ teaspoon salt
- 1 teaspoon keto tomato sauce
- 1 teaspoon olive oil
- ¼ teaspoon minced garlic
- ¼ teaspoon onion powder
- 1 teaspoon dried cilantro
- ½ teaspoon ground cumin
- 2 oz avocado, chopped
- 2 big cabbage leaves, steamed
- 2 tablespoons water

1. Preheat the air fryer to 360°F.
2. In the mixing bowl mix up ground beef, salt, ground black pepper, tomato sauce, olive oil, minced garlic, onion powder, dried cilantro, water, and ground cumin.
3. Then add jalapeno and stir gently.
4. Transfer the ground beef mixture in the preheated air fryer basket.
5. Cook the meat mixture for 15 minutes.
6. Stir it with the help of the spatula after 8 minutes of cooking.
7. Then place the mixture over the cabbage leaves.
8. Top the ground beef with chopped avocado and roll into the burritos.

PER SERVING

Calories: 230| Fat: 15.9| Fiber: 9.3 |Carbs 15.9| Protein: 10.4

Cinnamon French Toast

Prep time: 12 minutes | Cook time: 9 minutes | Serves 2

- 1/3 cup almond flour
- 1 egg, beaten
- ¼ teaspoon baking powder
- 2 teaspoons Erythritol
- ¼ teaspoon vanilla extract
- 1 teaspoon cream cheese
- ¼ teaspoon ground cinnamon
- 1 teaspoon ghee, melted

1. In the mixing bowl mix up almond flour, baking powder, and ground cinnamon.
2. Then add egg, vanilla extract, ghee, and cream cheese.
3. Stir the mixture with the help of the fork until homogenous.
4. Line the mugs bottom with baking paper.
5. After this, transfer the almond flour mixture in the mugs and flatten well.
6. Then preheat the air fryer to 355F.
7. Place the mugs with toasts in the air fryer basket and cook them for 9 minutes.
8. When the time is finished and the toasts are cooked, cool them little.
9. Then sprinkle the toasts with Erythritol.

PER SERVING

Calories: 85| Fat: 7.2| Fiber: 0.7| Carbs: 1.8| Protein: 3.9

Mushroom Fritters

Prep time: 10 minutes | Cook time: 6 minutes | Serves 2

- 1 cup mushrooms, grinded
- 1 teaspoon garlic powder
- 1 egg, beaten
- 3 teaspoons coconut flour
- ½ teaspoon chili powder
- 1 teaspoon coconut oil
- 1 tablespoon almond flour

1. In the mixing bowl, mix mushrooms with garlic powder, egg, coconut flour, chili powder, and almond flour.
2. Make the mushroom fritters and put them in the air fryer basket.
3. Add coconut oil and cook the fritters at 400F for 3 minutes per side.

PER SERVING

Calories: 139 | Fat: 8.2g | Fiber: 5.6g | Carbs: 10.2g | Protein: 7.2 g

Seed Porridge

Prep time: 10 minutes | Cook time: 12 minutes | Serves 3

- 1 tablespoon butter
- ¼ teaspoon nutmeg
- 1/3 cup heavy cream
- 1 egg
- ¼ teaspoon salt
- 3 tablespoons sesame seeds
- 3 tablespoons chia seeds

1. Place the butter in your air fryer basket tray. Add the chia seeds, sesame seeds, heavy cream, nutmeg, and salt. Stir gently. Beat the egg in a cup and whisk it with a fork. Add the whisked egg to air fryer basket tray. Stir the mixture with a wooden spatula. Preheat your air fryer to 375°F.
2. Place the air fryer basket tray into air fryer and cook the porridge for 12-minutes. Stir it about 3 times during the cooking process. Remove the porridge from air fryer basket tray immediately and serve hot!

PER SERVING

Calories: 275 | Total Fat: 22.5g | Carbs: 13.2g | Protein: 7.9g

Breakfast Chicken Hash

Prep time: 10 minutes | Cook time: 14 minutes | Serves 3

- 6-ounces of cauliflower, chopped
- 7-ounce chicken fillet
- 1 tablespoon water
- 1 green pepper, chopped
- ½ yellow onion, diced
- 1 teaspoon ground black pepper
- 3 tablespoons butter
- 1 tablespoon cream

1. Chop the cauliflower and place into the blender and blend it carefully until you get cauliflower rice. Chop the chicken fillet into small pieces. Sprinkle the chicken fillet with ground black pepper and stir. Chop the chicken fillet into small pieces.
2. Preheat your air fryer to 380°F. Dice the yellow onion and chop the green pepper. In a large mixing bowl, combine ingredients, then add mixture to fryer basket. Then cook and serve chicken hash warm!

PER SERVING

Calories: 261 | Total Fat: 16.8g | Carbs: 7.1g | Protein: 21g

Greek Bread

Prep time: 15 minutes | Cook time: 4 minutes | Serves 6

- 1 cup Mozzarella, shredded
- 2 tablespoons Greek yogurt
- 1 egg, beaten
- ½ teaspoon baking powder
- ½ cup almond flour
- 1 teaspoon butter, melted

1. In the glass bowl mix up Mozzarella and yogurt.
2. Microwave the mixture for 2 minutes.
3. After this, mix up baking powder, almond flour, and egg.
4. Combine together the almond flour mixture and melted Mozzarella mixture.
5. Stir it with the help of the spatula until smooth.
6. Refrigerate the dough for 10 minutes.
7. Then cut it on 6 pieces and roll up to get the flatbread pieces.
8. Air fryer the bread for 3 minutes at 400F.
9. Then brush it with melted butter and cook for 1 minute more or until the bread is light brown.

PER SERVING

Calories: 43| Fat: 3.4| Fiber: 0.3| Carbs: 0.9| Protein: 2.8

Cod Sticks

Prep time: 15 minutes | Cook time: 6 minutes | Serves 2

- 10 oz cod fillet
- ¼ cup almond flour
- 1 tablespoon coconut flour
- 1 egg white
- 1 teaspoon dried oregano
- ½ teaspoon onion powder
- ½ teaspoon salt
- 1 teaspoon avocado oil

1. Chop the cod fillet and put it in the blender.
2. Add coconut flour, egg white, dried oregano, salt, and onion powder.
3. Blend the mixture until smooth.
4. Then make the medium sticks from the fish mixture and coat them in the almond flour.
5. Brush the air fryer basket with avocado oil.
6. Then place the cod sticks in the air fryer in one layer.
7. Cook the fish sticks for 6 minutes at 400F.
8. Flip the fish sticks after 3 minutes of cooking.

PER SERVING

Calories: 167| Fat: 4.1| Fiber: 2.3| Carbs: 4.2| Protein: 28.8

Garlic Bread

Prep time:10 minutes |Cook time: 8 minutes |Serves 4

- 1 oz Mozzarella, shredded
- 2 tablespoons almond flour
- 1 teaspoon cream cheese
- ¼ teaspoon garlic powder
- ¼ teaspoon baking powder
- 1 egg, beaten
- 1 teaspoon coconut oil, melted
- ¼ teaspoon minced garlic
- 1 teaspoon dried dill
- 1 oz Provolone cheese, grated

1. In the mixing bowl mix up Mozzarella, almond flour, cream cheese, garlic powder, baking powder, egg, minced garlic, dried dill, and Provolone cheese.
2. When the mixture is homogenous, transfer it on the baking paper and spread it in the shape of the bread.
3. Sprinkle the garlic bread with coconut oil.
4. Preheat the air fryer to 400F.
5. Transfer the baking paper with garlic bread in the air fryer and cook for 8 minutes or until it is light brown.
6. When the garlic bread is cooked, cut it on 4 servings and place it in the serving plates.

PER SERVING

Calories: 155| Fat: 12.7| Fiber: 1.6| Carbs: 4| Protein: 8.3

Cheese Muffins

Prep time: 10 minutes | Cook time: 10 minutes | Serves 6

- 1 cup ground chicken
- ½ cup Cheddar cheese, shredded
- 1 teaspoon dried oregano
- ½ teaspoon salt
- 1 tablespoon butter, softened
- 1 teaspoon dried parsley
- 2 tablespoons coconut flour

1. Mix all ingredients in the mixing bowl and stir until homogenous.
2. Then pour the muffin mixture in the muffin molds and transfer the molds in the air fryer.
3. Bake the muffins at 375°F for 10 minutes.

PER SERVING

Calories: 110 | Fat: 7.1g | Fiber: 1.1g | Carbs: 2g | Protein: 9.5 g

Kale Omelet

Prep time:10 minutes |Cook time: 20 minutes |Serves 4

- 1 eggplant, cubed
- 4 eggs, whisked
- 2 teaspoons cilantro, chopped
- Salt and black pepper to the taste
- ½ teaspoon Italian seasoning Cooking spray
- ½ cup kale, chopped
- 2 tablespoons cheddar, grated
- 2 tablespoons fresh basil, chopped

1. In a bowl, mix all the ingredients except the cooking spray and whisk well.
2. Grease a pan that fits your air fryer with the cooking spray, pour the eggs mix, spread, put the pan in the machine and cook at 370 °F for 20 minutes.
3. Divide the mix between plates and serve for breakfast.

PER SERVING

Calories: 241| Fat: 11| Fiber: 4| Carbs: 5| Protein: 12

The Low-Carb Air Fryer Cookbook

Chicken Muffins

Prep time: 10 minutes | Cook time: 10 minutes | Serves 6

- 1 cup ground chicken
- 1 cup ground pork
- ½ cup Mozzarella, shredded
- 1 teaspoon dried oregano
- ½ teaspoon salt
- 1 teaspoon ground paprika
- ½ teaspoon white pepper
- 1 tablespoon ghee, melted
- 1 teaspoon dried dill
- 2 tablespoons almond flour
- 1 egg, beaten

1. In the bowl mix up ground chicken, ground pork, dried oregano, salt, ground paprika, white pepper, dried dill, almond flour, and egg.
2. Then brush the silicone muffin molds with melted ghee.
3. Put the meat mixture in the muffin molds.
4. Flatten the surface of every muffin with the help of the spoon and top with remaining Mozzarella.
5. Preheat the air fryer to 375°F.
6. Then arrange the muffins in the air fryer basket and cook them for 10 minutes.
7. Cool the cooked muffins to the room temperature and remove from the muffin molds.

PER SERVING

Calories: 291| Fat: 20.6| Fiber: 1.3| Carbs: 2.7| Protein: 23.9

Sausage Bake

Prep time: 15 minutes | Cook time: 23 minutes | Serves 6

- 2 jalapeno peppers, sliced
- 7 oz ground sausages
- 1 teaspoon dill seeds
- 3 oz Colby Jack Cheese, shredded
- 4 eggs, beaten
- 1 tablespoon cream cheese
- ½ teaspoon salt
- 1 teaspoon butter, softened
- 1 teaspoon olive oil

1. Preheat the skillet well and pour the olive oil inside.
2. Then add ground sausages, salt, and cook the mixture for 5-8 minutes over the medium heat Stir it from time to time.
3. Meanwhile, preheat the air fryer to 400F.
4. Grease the air fryer basket with softened butter and place the cooked ground sausages inside.
5. Flatten the mixture and top with the sliced jalapeno peppers.
6. Then add shredded cheese.
7. In the mixing bowl mix up eggs and cream cheese.
8. Pour the liquid over the cheese.
9. Sprinkle the casserole with dill seeds.
10. The cooking time of the casserole is 16 minutes at 400F.
11. You can increase the cooking time if you prefer the crunchy crust.

PER SERVING

Calories: 230| Fat: 18.9| Fiber: 0.3| Carbs: 1.3| Protein: 13.4

Tofu Wraps

Prep time: 15 minutes | Cook time: 9 minutes | Serves 4

- 4 low carb tortillas
- 5 oz tofu, cubed
- 1 teaspoon mustard
- 1 teaspoon avocado oil
- 1 teaspoon lemon juice
- ½ cup white cabbage, shredded
- 4 teaspoons cream cheese
- 2 chipotles, chopped

1. Preheat the air fryer to 400F.
2. Meanwhile, mix up mustard with avocado oil and lemon juice.
3. Then place the tofu on the tortillas.
4. Add shredded cabbage, chipotles, and cream cheese.
5. Fold the wraps.

PER SERVING

Calories: 133| Fat: 5.1| Fiber: 8.1| Carbs: 15.7| Protein: 6.9

Coriander Sausages Muffins

Prep time: 10 minutes | Cook time: 12 minutes | Serves 4

- 4 teaspoons coconut flour
- 1 tablespoon coconut cream
- 1 egg, beaten
- ½ teaspoon baking powder
- 6 oz sausage meat
- 1 teaspoon spring onions, chopped
- ½ teaspoon ground coriander
- 1 teaspoon sesame oil
- ½ teaspoon salt

1. In the mixing bowl mix up coconut flour, coconut cream, egg, baking powder, minced onion, and ground coriander.
2. Add salt and whisk the mixture until smooth.
3. After this, add the sausage meat and stir the muffin batter.
4. Preheat the air fryer to 385F.
5. Brush the muffin molds with sesame oil and pour the batter inside.
6. Place the rack in the air fryer basket.
7. Put the muffins on a rack.
8. Cook the meal for 12 minutes.

PER SERVING

Calories: 239| Fat: 17.2| Fiber: 5.1| Carbs: 8.7| Protein: 11.7

Mozzarella Swirls

Prep time: 15 minutes | Cook time: 12 minutes | Serves 6

- 2 tablespoons almond flour
- 1 tablespoon coconut flour
- ½ cup Mozzarella cheese, shredded
- 1 teaspoon Truvia
- 2 tablespoons butter, softened
- ¼ teaspoon baking powder
- 1 egg, beaten
- Cooking spray

1. In the bowl mix up almond flour, coconut flour, Mozzarella cheese, Truvia, butter, baking powder, and egg.
2. Knead the soft and non-sticky dough.
3. Then preheat the air fryer to 355F.
4. Place the cheese swirls in the air fryer in one layer and cook them for 12 minutes or until they are light brown.
5. Repeat the same step with remaining uncooked dough.
6. It is recommended to serve the cheese Danish warm.

PER SERVING

Calories: 115| Fat: 10| Fiber: 2| Carbs: 3.9| Protein: 4

The Low-Carb Air Fryer Cookbook

Chicken and Cream Lasagna

Prep time: 10 minutes | **Cook time:** 25 minutes | **Serves 2**

- 1 egg, beaten
- 1 tablespoon heavy cream
- 1 teaspoon cream cheese
- 2 tablespoons almond flour
- ¼ teaspoon salt
- ¼ cup coconut cream
- 1 teaspoon dried basil
- 1 teaspoon keto tomato sauce
- ¼ cup Mozzarella, shredded
- 1 teaspoon butter, melted
- ½ cup ground chicken

1. Make the lasagna batter: in the bowl mix up egg, heavy cream, cream cheese, and almond flour.
2. Add coconut cream.
3. Stir the liquid until smooth.
4. Then preheat the air fryer to 355F.
5. Brush the air fryer basket with butter.
6. Pour ½ part of lasagna batter in the air fryer basket and flatten it in one layer.
7. Then in the separated bowl mix up tomato sauce, basil, salt, and ground chicken.
8. Put the chicken mixture over the batter in the air fryer.
9. Add beaten egg.
10. Then top it with remaining lasagna batter and sprinkle with shredded Mozzarella.
11. Cook the lasagna for 25 minutes.

PER SERVING

Calories: 388| Fat: 31.8| Fiber: 3.8| Carbs: 8.7| Protein: 21

Cheddar Pancakes

Prep time: 10 minutes | **Cook time:** 7 minutes | **Serves 2**

- 2 tablespoons almond flour
- ¼ teaspoon baking powder
- 1 teaspoon Erythritol
- 1 teaspoon cream cheese
- 1 teaspoon butter, melted
- 2 eggs, beaten
- 1 bacon slice, cooked, cut into halves
- 1 Cheddar cheese slice
- 1 teaspoon sesame oil

1. Make the pancake batter: in the mixing bowl mix up baking powder, almond flour, Erythritol, cream cheese, and 1 beaten egg.
2. Preheat the air fryer to 400F.
3. Then line the air fryer with baking paper.
4. Then flip the pancake on another side and cook for 1 minute more.
5. Repeat the same steps with the remaining pancake batter.
6. You should get 4 pancakes.
7. After this, brush the air fryer basket with sesame oil.
8. Pour the remaining beaten egg in the air fryer and cook it for 3 minutes at 390F.
9. Cut the cooked egg into 2 parts.
10. Place the 1 half of cooked egg on the one pancake.
11. Top it with 1 half of the bacon and second pancake.

PER SERVING

Calories: 374| Fat: 31.7| Fiber: 3| Carbs: 7| Protein: 18.7

The Low-Carb Air Fryer Cookbook

Chapter 3

Poultry

Chicken and Arugula Salad

Prep time: 15 minutes | Cook time: 12 minutes | Serves 2

- 2 bacon slices, cooked, chopped
- 2 cups arugula, chopped
- 10 oz chicken breast, skinless, boneless
- 1 teaspoon ground black pepper
- ½ teaspoon salt
- 1 teaspoon avocado oil
- ½ teaspoon ground cumin
- ½ teaspoon ground paprika
- 1 tablespoon olive oil
- ¼ teaspoon minced garlic
- 1 teaspoon fresh cilantro, chopped

1. Rub the chicken breast with ground black pepper, salt, ground cumin, ground paprika, and avocado oil.
2. Then preheat the air fryer to 365°F.
3. Put the chicken breast in the preheated air fryer and cook for 12 minutes.
4. Meanwhile, in the salad bowl mix up chopped bacon, arugula, and fresh cilantro.
5. In the shallow bowl mix up minced garlic and olive oil.
6. Chop the cooked chicken breasts and add in the salad mixture.
7. Sprinkle the salad with garlic oil and shake well.

PER SERVING

Calories: 339| Fat: 19.1| Fiber: 1| Carbs: 2.5| Protein: 37.9

Parsley Turkey Stew

Prep time: 5 minutes | Cook time: 25 minutes | Serves 4

- 1 turkey breast, skinless, boneless and cubed
- 1 tablespoon olive oil
- 1 broccoli head, florets separated
- 1 cup keto tomato sauce
- Salt and black pepper to the taste
- 1 tablespoon parsley, chopped

1. In a baking dish that fits your air fryer, mix the turkey with the rest of the ingredients except the parsley, toss, introduce the dish in the fryer, bake at 380 °F for 25 minutes, divide into bowls, sprinkle the parsley on top and serve.

PER SERVING

Calories: 250| Fat: 11| Fiber: 2| Carbs: 6| Protein: 12

Chili Chicken Cutlets

Prep time: 20 minutes | Cook time: 16 minutes | Serves 4

- 15 oz chicken fillet
- 1 teaspoon white pepper
- 1 teaspoon ghee, melted
- ½ teaspoon onion powder
- ¼ teaspoon chili flakes

1. Chop the chicken fillet into the tiny pieces.
2. Then sprinkle the chopped chicken with white pepper, onion powder, and chili flakes.
3. Stir the mixture until homogenous.
4. Make the medium-size cutlets from the mixture.
5. Preheat the air fryer to 365°F.
6. Brush the air fryer basket with ghee and put the chicken cutlets inside.
7. Cook them for 8 minutes and then flip on another side with the help of the spatula.
8. Transfer the cooked chicken cutlets on the serving plate.

PER SERVING

Calories: 214| Fat: 9| Fiber: 0.2| Carbs: 0.6| Protein: 30.9

Pickled Poultry

Prep time: 10 minutes | Cook time: 25 minutes | Serves 4

- 600g of poultry, without bones or skin
- 3 white onions, peeled and cut into thin slices
- 5 garlic cloves, peeled and sliced
- 3 dl olive oil
- 1 dl apple cider vinegar
- 1/2 l white wine
- 2 bay leaves
- 5 g peppercorns
- Flour
- Pepper
- Salt

1. Rub the bird in dice that we will pepper and flour
2. Put oil in the prepared pan and heat. When the oil is hot, fry the floured meat dice in it until golden brown.
3. Take them out and reserve, placing them in a clay or oven dish. Strain the oil in which you have fried the meat
4. Preheat the oven to 170° C
5. Put the already cast oil in another pan over the fire. Sauté the garlic and onions in it. Add the white wine and let cook about 3 minutes.
6. Remove the pan from the heat, add the vinegar to the oil and wine. Remove, rectify salt, and pour this mixture into the source where you had left the bird dice.
7. Put in the oven, lower the temperature to 140°C and bake for 1 and 1/2 hours. Remove the source from the oven and let it stand at room temperature
8. When the source is cold, put it in the fridge and let it rest a few hours before serving.

PER SERVING

Calories:232 | Fat:15g |Carbs: 5.89g | Protein: 18.2g

Cream Cheese Chicken

Prep time: 10 minutes | Cook time: 25 minutes | Serves 5

- 1½-pound chicken breast, skinless, boneless
- 1 teaspoon ground paprika
- ½ teaspoon ground turmeric
- 2 teaspoons cream cheese
- 1 oz scallions, chopped
- 1 teaspoon avocado oil
- ½ teaspoon salt

1. Rub the chicken breast with ground paprika, turmeric, and salt.
2. Then put the chicken in the air fryer basket.
3. Add avocado oil, scallions, and cream cheese.
4. Cook the meal at 375°F for 25 minutes.

PER SERVING

Calories: 165 | Fat: 4.1g | Fiber: 0.4g | Carbs: 0.9g | Protein: 29.1 g

Provolone Meatballs

Prep time: 10 minutes | Cook time: 12 minutes | Serves 6

- 12 oz ground chicken
- ½ cup coconut flour
- 2 egg whites, whisked
- 1 teaspoon ground black pepper
- 1 egg yolk
- 1 teaspoon salt
- 4 oz Provolone cheese, grated
- 1 teaspoon ground oregano
- ½ teaspoon chili powder
- 1 tablespoon avocado oil

1. In the mixing bowl mix up ground chicken, ground black pepper, egg yolk, salt, Provolone cheese, ground oregano, and chili powder.
2. Stir the mixture until homogenous and make the small meatballs.
3. Dip the meatballs in the whisked egg whites and coat in the coconut flour.
4. Preheat the air fryer to 370F.
5. Put the chicken meatballs in the air fryer basket and cook them for 6 minutes from both sides.

PER SERVING

Calories: 234| Fat: 11.7| Fiber: 3.7| Carbs: 6.6| Protein: 24.3

Long-Roasted Chicken Thighs

Prep time: 10 minutes | Cook time: 180 minutes | Serves 4

- Kosher salt
- 8 skin-on, bone-in chicken thighs
- 4 cloves of garlic (should be sliced)
- 4 bay leaves, torn in half
- Black pepper

1. Season the chicken a day or two before you cook this recipe.
2. Sprinkle some salt on both sides of the chicken thighs.
3. Mix the garlic, bay leaves, and black pepper together. Coat the chicken thighs in the mixture before you refrigerate them for at least 24 hours.
4. Reduce the heat to 325 °F and cook it for another 1 hour. This will make the chicken thighs crispy, but they will also shrink in size. They will be golden brown.
5. You can now serve them with vegetable salad.

PER SERVING

Calories: 225 | Fat: 14g | Carbs: 3g | Protein: 20g

Stuffed Turkey

Prep time: 15 minutes | Cook time: 30 minutes | Serves 4

- 2-pound turkey fillet
- 1 cup mushrooms, chopped
- 1 teaspoon garlic powder
- 2 oz scallions, chopped
- 1 tablespoon coconut oil
- 1 teaspoon olive oil
- 1 teaspoon chili powder

1. Mix chili powder with mushrooms, garlic powder, olive oil, and scallions.
2. Then make the cut in the shape of pocket in the turkey fillet. Fill it with mushroom mixture and secure the cut with the help of the toothpick.
3. Grease the air fryer basket with coconut oil and put the stuffed turkey inside.
4. Cook it at 380f for 30 minutes.

PER SERVING

Calories: 266 | Fat: 5.8g | Fiber: 0.8g | Carbs: 2.5g | Protein: 48.1 g

Spicy Chicken Roll

Prep time: 15 minutes | Cook time: 25 minutes | Serves 5

- 1-pound chicken fillet
- 1 teaspoon cayenne pepper
- 1 oz scallions, chopped
- 1 oz Parmesan, grated
- ½ teaspoon dried basil
- ½ teaspoon olive oil
- ½ teaspoon chili powder

1. Beat the chicken fillet with the help of the kitchen hammer to get the flat cutlet.
2. Then rub it with cayenne pepper, dried basil, olive oil, and chili powder.
3. Top the chicken fillet with Parmesan and scallions and roll into a roll.
4. Put it in the air fryer basket and cook it for 25 minutes at 385F.

PER SERVING

Calories: 198 | Fat: 8.5g | Fiber: 0.3g | Carbs: 1g | Protein: 28.2 g

Oregano Duck Spread

Prep time: 15 minutes | Cook time: 10 minutes | Serves 6

- ½ cup butter, softened
- 12 oz duck liver
- 1 tablespoon sesame oil
- 1 teaspoon salt
- 1 tablespoon dried oregano
- ½ onion, peeled

1. Preheat the air fryer to 395F.
2. Chop the onion.
3. Put the duck liver in the air fryer, add onion, and cook the ingredients for 10 minutes.
4. Then transfer the duck pate in the food processor and process it for 2-3 minutes or until the liver is smooth (it depends on the food processor power).
5. Then add onion and blend the mixture for 2 minutes more.
6. Transfer the liver mixture into the bowl.
7. After this, add oregano, salt, sesame oil, and butter.
8. Stir the duck liver with the help of the spoon and transfer it in the bowl.
9. Refrigerate the pate for 10-20 minutes before serving.

PER SERVING

Calories: 227 | Fat: 20.4 | Fiber: 0.5 | Carbs: 1.8 | Protein: 9.9

Rosemary Chicken Stew

Prep time: 5 minutes | Cook time: 20 minutes | Serves 4

- 2 cups okra
- 2 garlic cloves, minced
- 1 pound chicken breasts, skinless, boneless and cubed
- 4 tomatoes, cubed
- 1 tablespoon olive oil
- 1 teaspoon rosemary, dried
- Salt and black pepper to the taste
- 1 tablespoon parsley, chopped

1. Heat up a pan that fits your air fryer with the oil over medium-high heat, add the chicken, garlic, rosemary, salt and pepper, toss and brown for 5 minutes.
2. Add the remaining ingredients, toss again, place the pan in the air fryer and cook at 380 °F for 15 minutes more.
3. Divide the stew into bowls and serve for lunch.

PER SERVING

Calories: 220 | Fat: 13 | Fiber: 3 | Carbs: 5 | Protein: 11

Turkey Breast

Prep time: 20 minutes | Cook time: 35 minutes |Serves 2

- 4 pound of turkey breast, with the rib removed
- 2 teaspoons of kosher salt
- 1/2 tablespoon of dry turkey or poultry seasoning
- 1 tablespoon of olive oil

1. Coat the turkey breast with 1/2 tablespoon of oil.
2. The next step is to season both sides of the turkey breast with salt and turkey seasoning. You can add the remaining oil to the seasoned turkey.
3. Preheat your air fryer to 350 °F before cooking the turkey for 20 minutes.
4. Turn it over and cook it at 160 °F for another 30 to 35 minutes.
5. Let it cool for 10 minutes before you carve it.

PER SERVING

Calories:226| Fat:10g |Carbs: 0.3g | Protein: 32.5g

Coated Chicken

Prep time: 15 minutes | Cook time: 20 minutes | Serves 6

- 3-pounds chicken breast, skinless, boneless
- 1 tablespoon coconut shred
- 2 tablespoons pork rinds
- 1 teaspoon ground black pepper
- 2 eggs, beaten
- 1 tablespoon avocado oil

1. In the shallow bowl, mix coconut shred with pork rinds, and ground black pepper.
2. Then cut the chicken breasts into 6 servings and dip in the eggs.
3. Coat the chicken in the coconut shred mixture and put it in the air fryer basket.
4. Then sprinkle the chicken with avocado oil and cook at 380F for 20 minutes.

PER SERVING

Calories: 305 | Fat: 8.7g | Fiber: 0.3g | Carbs: 1.1g | Protein: 52.2 g

Buttery Chicken Wings

Prep time:5 minutes |Cook time: 30 minutes |Serves 4

- 2 pounds chicken wings
- Salt and black pepper to the taste
- 3 garlic cloves, minced
- 3 tablespoons butter, melted
- ½ cup heavy cream
- ½ teaspoon basil, dried
- ½ teaspoon oregano, dried
- ¼ cup parmesan, grated

1. In a baking dish that fits your air fryer, mix the chicken wings with all the ingredients except the parmesan and toss.
2. Put the dish to your air fryer and cook at 380 °F for 30 minutes.
3. Sprinkle the cheese on top, leave the mix aside for 10 minutes, divide between plates and serve.

PER SERVING

Calories: 270| Fat: 12| Fiber: 3| Carbs: 6| Protein: 17

The Low-Carb Air Fryer Cookbook

Chicken and Asparagus

Prep time: 5 minutes | Cook time: 20 minutes | Serves 4

- 4 chicken breasts, skinless, boneless and halved
- 1 tablespoon sweet paprika
- 1 bunch asparagus, trimmed and halved
- 1 tablespoon olive oil
- Salt and black pepper to the taste

1. In a bowl, mix all the ingredients, toss, put them in your Air Fryer's basket and cook at 390 °F for 20 minutes.
2. Divide between plates and serve for lunch.

PER SERVING

Calories: 230| Fat: 11| Fiber: 3| Carbs: 5| Protein: 12

Sun-dried Tomatoes and Chicken Mix

Prep time: 5 minutes | Cook time: 25 minutes | Serves 4

- 4 chicken thighs, skinless, boneless
- 1 tablespoon olive oil Apinch of salt and black pepper
- 1 tablespoon thyme, chopped
- 1 cup chicken stock
- 3 garlic cloves, minced
- ½ cup coconut cream
- 1 cup sun-dried tomatoes, chopped
- 4 tablespoons parmesan, grated

1. Heat up a pan that fits the air fryer with the oil over medium-high heat, add the chicken, salt, pepper and the garlic, and brown for 2-3 minutes on each side.
2. Add the rest of the ingredients except the parmesan, toss, put the pan in the air fryer and cook at 370 °F for 20 minutes.
3. Sprinkle the parmesan on top, leave the mix aside for 5 minutes, divide everything between plates and serve.

PER SERVING

Calories: 275| Fat: 12| Fiber: 4| Carbs: 6| Protein: 17

Sweet and Sour Chicken Drumsticks

Prep time: 10 minutes | Cook time: 30 minutes | Serves 4

- 1 tablespoon keto tomato paste
- 2 tablespoons avocado oil
- 2 tablespoons coconut aminos
- 1 teaspoon garlic powder
- 1 teaspoon chili flakes
- 2-pounds chicken drumsticks
- 1 teaspoon Erythritol

1. Sprinkle the chicken drumsticks with tomato paste, avocado oil, coconut aminos, garlic powder, chili flakes, and Erythritol.
2. Put them in the air fryer and cook at 360°F for 15 minutes per side.

PER SERVING

Calories: 401 | Fat: 13.9g | Fiber: 0.6g | Carbs: 2.2g | Protein: 62.8 g

The Low-Carb Air Fryer Cookbook

Oregano and Lemon Chicken Drumsticks

Prep time: 15 minutes | Cook time: 21 minutes | Serves 4

- 4 chicken drumsticks, with skin, bone-in
- 1 teaspoon dried cilantro
- ½ teaspoon dried oregano
- ½ teaspoon salt
- 1 teaspoon lemon juice
- 1 teaspoon butter, softened
- 2 garlic cloves, diced

1. In the mixing bowl mix up dried cilantro, oregano, and salt.
2. Then fill the chicken drumstick's skin with a cilantro mixture.
3. Add butter and diced garlic.
4. Sprinkle the chicken with lemon juice.
5. Preheat the air fryer to 375°F.
6. Put the chicken drumsticks in the air fryer and cook them for 21 minutes.

PER SERVING

Calories: 89| Fat: 3.6| Fiber: 0.1| Carbs: 0.7| Protein: 12.8

Asparagus Chicken

Prep time: 15 minutes | Cook time: 25 minutes | Serves 4

- 1 cup asparagus, chopped
- 1-pound chicken thighs, skinless, boneless
- 1 teaspoon onion powder
- 1 oz scallions, chopped
- 1 tablespoon coconut oil, melted
- 1 teaspoon smoked paprika

1. Mix chicken thighs with onion powder, coconut oil, and smoked paprika.
2. Put the chicken thighs in the air fryer and cook at 385F for 20 minutes.
3. Then flip the chicken thighs on another side and top with chopped asparagus and scallions.
4. Cook the meal for 5 minutes more.

PER SERVING

Calories: 257 | Fat: 11.9g | Fiber: 1.1g | Carbs: 2.6g | Protein: 33.8 g

Chicken with Asparagus and Zucchini

Prep time: 15 minutes | Cook time: 25 minutes | Serves 4

- 1 pound chicken thighs, boneless and skinless
- Juice of 1 lemon
- 2 tablespoons olive oil
- 3 garlic cloves, minced
- 1 teaspoon oregano, dried
- 1 zucchinis, halved lengthwise and sliced into half-moons

1. In a bowl, mix the chicken with all the ingredients except the asparagus and the zucchinis, toss and leave aside for 15 minutes.
2. Add the zucchinis and the asparagus, toss, put everything into a pan that fits the air fryer, and cook at 380 °F for 25 minutes.
3. Divide everything between plates and serve.

PER SERVING

Calories: 280| Fat: 11| Fiber: 4| Carbs: 6| Protein: 17

Lemon Chicken Mix

Prep time: 15 minutes | Cook time: 15 minutes | Serves 3

- 4 chicken thighs, skinless, boneless
- 1 tablespoon lemon juice
- 1 teaspoon ground paprika
- ½ teaspoon salt
- ½ teaspoon ground black pepper
- 1 tablespoon sesame oil
- ½ teaspoon dried parsley
- ½ teaspoon keto tomato sauce

1. Cut the chicken thighs into halves and put them in the bowl.
2. Add lemon juice, ground paprika, salt, ground black pepper, sesame oil, parsley, and tomato sauce.
3. Mix up the chicken with the help of the fingertips and leave for 10-15 minutes to marinate.
4. Then string the meat on the wooden skewers and put in the preheated to 375°F air fryer.
5. Cook the tavuk shish for 10 minutes at 375°F.
6. Then flip the meal on another side and cook for 5 minutes more.

PER SERVING

Calories: 415| Fat: 19.1| Fiber: 0.4| Carbs: 0.9| Protein: 56.6

Chapter 4

Beef, Pork and Lamb

Beef Pie

Prep time: 25 minutes | Cook time: 6 minutes | Serves 4

- 2 cup cauliflower, boiled, mashed
- 2 oz celery stalk, chopped
- 1 cup ground beef
- ½ teaspoon salt
- ½ teaspoon ground turmeric
- 1 tablespoon coconut oil
- ½ teaspoon avocado oil
- 1 teaspoon dried parsley
- 1 tablespoon keto tomato sauce
- 1 garlic clove, diced

1. Toss the coconut oil in the skillet and melt it over the medium heat.
2. Then add celery stalk.
3. Cook the vegetables for 5 minutes.
4. Stir them from time to time.
5. Meanwhile, brush the air fryer pan with avocado oil.
6. Transfer the cooked vegetables in the pan and flatten them in the shape of the layer.
7. Then put the ground beef in the pan.
8. Add salt, parsley, and turmeric.
9. Cook the ground meat for 10 minutes over the medium heat.
10. Stir it from time to time.
11. Add tomato sauce and stir well.
12. After this, transfer the ground beef over the vegetables.
13. Then add garlic and top the pie with mashed cauliflower mash.
14. Preheat the air fryer to 360°F.
15. Put the pan with shepherd pie in the air fryer and cook for 6 minutes or until you get the crunchy crust.

PER SERVING

Calories: 116| Fat: 7.7| Fiber: 1.9| Carbs: 4.5| Protein: 7.8

Zucchini Pasta

Prep time: 15 minutes | Cook time: 14 minutes | Serves 4

- ½ cup ground beef
- ¼ teaspoon salt
- ½ teaspoon chili flakes
- ¼ teaspoon dried dill
- 2 zucchinis, trimmed
- 2 tablespoons mascarpone
- 1 teaspoon olive oil
- ½ teaspoon ground black pepper
- Cooking spray

1. In the mixing bowl mix up ground beef, salt, chili flakes, and dill.
2. Then make the small meatballs.
3. Preheat the air fryer to 365°F.
4. Spray the air fryer basket with cooking spray and place the meatballs inside in one layer.
5. Cook the meatballs for 12 minutes.
6. Shake them after 6 minutes of cooking to avoid burning.
7. Then remove the meatballs from the air fryer.
8. with the help of the spiralizer make the zucchini noodles and sprinkle them with olive oil and ground black pepper.
9. Place the zucchini noodles in the air place the meatballs inside in one layer. fryer and cook them for 2 minutes at 400F.
10. Then mix up zucchini noodles and mascarpone and transfer them in the serving plates.
11. Top the noodles with cooked meatballs.

PER SERVING

Calories: 145| Fat: 8.8| Fiber: 2.3| Carbs: 7.5| Protein: 10.7

Cheddar Beef Chili

Prep time: 15 minutes | Cook time: 20 minutes | Serves 2

- 1 cup ground beef
- ¼ cup Cheddar cheese, shredded
- ¼ cup green beans, trimmed and halved
- ¼ cup spring onion, diced
- 1 teaspoon fresh cilantro, chopped
- 2 chili pepper, chopped
- 1 teaspoon ghee
- 1 tablespoon keto tomato sauce
- ½ cup chicken broth
- ½ teaspoon salt
- ¼ teaspoon garlic powder

1. Put ghee in the skillet and melt it.
2. Put the ground beef in the skillet.
3. Add spring onion, garlic powder, and salt.
4. Stir the ground beef mixture and cook it over the medium heat for 5 minutes.
5. Then transfer the mixture in the air fryer pan.
6. Then add green beans and cilantro.
7. Mix up the chili gently and top with Cheddar cheese.
8. Preheat the air fryer to 390F.
9. Put the pan with chili con carne in the air fryer and cook it for 10 minutes.

PER SERVING

Calories: 244| Fat: 15.5| Fiber: 1.7| Carbs: 6.4| Protein: 19.4

Pork Bowls

Prep time: 5 minutes | Cook time: 20 minutes | Serves 4

- ½ pound pork stew meat, cubed
- ¼ cup keto tomato sauce
- 1 tablespoon olive oil
- 2 cups mustard greens
- 1 yellow bell pepper, chopped
- 2 green onions, chopped
- Salt and black pepper to the taste

1. In a pan that fits your air fryer, mix all the ingredients, toss, introduce the pan in the air fryer and cook at 370 °F for 20 minutes.
2. Divide into bowls and serve for lunch.

PER SERVING

Calories: 265| Fat: 12| Fiber: 3| Carbs: 5| Protein: 14

Tender Meat Salad

Prep time: 10 minutes | Cook time: 25 minutes | Serves 4

- 1-pound beef sirloin, sliced
- 1 teaspoon white pepper
- ½ teaspoon salt
- 1 teaspoon coconut oil, melted
- 1 cup lettuce, chopped
- 2 pecans, chopped
- 1 tablespoon avocado oil

1. In the mixing bowl, mix beef sirloin with white pepper, salt, and coconut oil.
2. Then mix beef sirloin with lettuce, pecans, and avocado oil.
3. Shake the salad gently.

PER SERVING

Calories: 277 | Fat: 13.7g | Fiber: 1.1g | Carbs: 2g | Protein: 35.3 g

Stuffed Cabbage and Pork Loin Rolls

Prep time: 5 minutes | Cook time: 20 minutes | Serves 4

- 500 g. white cabbage
- 1 onion
- 8 pork tenderloin steaks
- 2 carrots
- 4 tbsp. soy sauce
- 50 g. extra virgin olive oil
- Salt to taste
- 8 sheets rice

1. Put the chopped cabbage in the Thermo mix glass together with the onion and the chopped carrot.
2. Select 5 seconds on the speed 5. Add the extra virgin olive oil. Select 5 minutes, left turn, and spoon speed.
3. Add the soy sauce. Select 5 minutes, room temperature, left turn, spoon speed. Rectify salt. Let it cold down.
4. Hydrate the rice slices. Extend and distribute the filling between them.
5. Make the rolls, folding so that the edges are completely closed. Set the rolls in the air fryer and paint with the oil.
6. Select 10 minutes for cooking time and set the temperature to 375°F.

PER SERVING

Calories: 119.5 | Fat: 3.1g | Carbs: 0g | Protein: 21.4g

Flavored Pork Chops

Prep time: 9 minutes | Cook time: 35 minutes | Serves 2

- 3 garlic cloves, ground
- 2 tbsp. olive oil
- 1 tbsp. marinade
- 4 thawed pork chops

1. Mix the cloves of ground garlic, marinade, and oil. Then apply this mixture to the chops.
2. Put the chops in the air fryer at 360°F for 35 minutes. Serve.

PER SERVING

Calories: 117.5 | Fat: 3.1g | Carbs: 0g | Protein: 22.5g

Dill Pork Shoulder

Prep time: 20 minutes | Cook time: 20 minutes | Serves 4

- 1-pound pork shoulder, boneless
- 3 spring onions, chopped
- 1 teaspoon dried dill
- 1 teaspoon keto tomato sauce
- 1 tablespoon water
- 1 teaspoon salt
- 2 tablespoons sesame oil
- 1 teaspoon ground black pepper
- ½ teaspoon garlic powder

1. In the shallow bowl mix up salt, ground black pepper, and garlic powder.
2. Then add dried dill.
3. Sprinkle the pork shoulder with a spice mixture from each side.
4. Then in the separated bowl, mix up tomato sauce, water, and sesame oil.
5. Brush the meat with the tomato mixture.
6. Then place it on the foil.
7. Add spring onions.
8. Wrap the pork shoulder.
9. Preheat the air fryer to 395F.
10. Put the wrapped pork shoulder in the air fryer basket and cook it for 20 minutes.
11. Let the cooked meat rest for 5-10 minutes and then discard the foil.

PER SERVING

Calories: 401 | Fat: 31.1 | Fiber: 0.5 | Carbs: 2.3 | Protein: 26.8

Cilantro Pork Meatballs

Prep time: 5 minutes | Cook time: 20 minutes | Serves 12

- 1 pound pork meat, ground
- 3 spring onions, minced
- 3 tablespoons cilantro, chopped
- 1 tablespoon ginger, grated
- 2 garlic cloves, minced
- 1 chili pepper, minced
- A pinch of salt and black pepper
- 1 and ½ tablespoons coconut aminos Cooking spray

1. In a bowl, mix all the ingredients except the cooking spray, stir really well and shape medium meatballs out of this mix.
2. Arrange them in your air fryer's basket, grease with cooking spray and cook at 380 °F for 20 minutes.
3. Serve as an appetizer.

PER SERVING

Calories: 200| Fat: 12| Fiber: 2| Carbs: 3| Protein: 14

Air Fryer Pork Satay

Prep time: 15 minutes | Cook time: 10 minutes | Serves 4

- 1 (1 lb./454 g.) pork tenderloin, cut into 1 1/2-inch cubes
- 1/4 cup onion, minced
- 2 garlic cloves, minced
- 1 jalapeño pepper, minced
- 2 tbsp. lime juice, freshly squeezed
- 2 tbsp. coconut milk
- 2 tbsp. unsalted peanut butter
- 2 tsp. curry powder

1. In a medium bowl, mix the pork, lime juice, garlic, onion, jalapeño, peanut butter, coconut milk, and curry powder until well combined. Let position for 10 minutes at room temperature.
2. Remove the pork from the marinade but reserve the marinade.
3. Thread the pork onto 8 skewers. Air fry at 380°F for 10 minutes, brushing once with the reserved marinade until the pork reaches at least 145°F on a meat thermometer.
4. Discard any remaining marinade and serve immediately.

PER SERVING

Calories: 194.5, Fats: 24.5g | Protein: 7.6g | Carbs: 1g| Fibers: 1g | Sugars: 2.5g

Stuffed Beef Roll

Prep time: 20 minutes | Cook time: 40 minutes | Serves 4

- 1-pound beef loin
- 2 oz mushrooms, chopped
- 1 teaspoon onion powder
- 1 oz bacon, chopped, cooked
- ½ teaspoon dried dill
- 1 teaspoon chili powder
- 1 tablespoon avocado oil
- ½ teaspoon cream cheese

1. Beat the beef loin with the help of the kitchen hammer to get the flat loin.
2. After this, mix mushrooms with onion powder, bacon, dried dill, chili powder, and cream cheese.
3. Put the mixture over the beef loin and roll it.
4. Secure the beef roll with toothpicks and brush with avocado oil.
5. Cook the beef roll at 370F for 40 minutes.

PER SERVING

Calories: 258 | Fat: 13.2g | Fiber: 0.6g | Carbs: 1.7g | Protein: 33.7 g

African Style Lamb

Prep time: 15 minutes | Cook time: 50 minutes | Serves 4

- 21 oz lamb cutlets
- 1 teaspoon white pepper
- 4 tablespoons avocado oil
- 1 teaspoon dried basil
- 1 tablespoon garlic powder
- 1 tablespoon ground coriander
- 1 tablespoon lemon zest, grated
- 3 tablespoons apple cider vinegar

1. Chop the lamb cutlets roughly and put in the air fryer.
2. Add all remaining ingredients and carefully mix the mixture.
3. Cook the meal at 365°F for 50 minutes. Stir it after 20 minutes of cooking.

PER SERVING

Calories: 307 | Fat: 12.7g | Fiber: 1.1g | Carbs: 3.1g | Protein: 42.4 g

Lamb Chops with Kalamata Spread

Prep time: 10 minutes | Cook time: 20 minutes | Serves 4

- 4 lamb chops
- 4 kalamata olives, diced
- 1 teaspoon minced garlic
- 1 cup fresh spinach, chopped
- 2 tablespoons olive oil
- 1 tablespoon lemon juice
- ½ teaspoon ground black pepper

1. Mix lamb chops with ground black pepper, lemon juice, and olive oil.
2. Put the lamb chops in the air fryer and cook them for 10 minutes per side at 360°F.
3. Meanwhile, blend all remaining ingredients until smooth.
4. Top the cooked lamb chops with olives spread.

PER SERVING

Calories: 228 | Fat: 13.8g | Fiber: 0.4g | Carbs: 1g | Protein: 24.2 g

Creamy Cheesy Bacon Dip

Prep time: 15 minutes | Cook time: 12 minutes | Serves 6

- 6 teaspoon cream cheese
- ½ cup heavy cream
- 1 teaspoon dried sage
- 1 cup Monterey Jack cheese, shredded
- ½ teaspoon chili flakes
- 1 tablespoon chives, chopped
- 1 teaspoon avocado oil
- ½ teaspoon salt
- 6 oz bacon, chopped

1. Preheat the air fryer to 400F.
2. Put the chopped bacon in the air fryer and cook it for 6 minutes.
3. Stir it after 3 minutes of cooking.
4. Clean the air fryer basket and insert the baking pan with bacon dip inside.
5. Cook it at 385F for 6 minutes.

PER SERVING

Calories: 271| Fat: 22.5| Fiber: 0| Carbs: 1| Protein: 15.6

Pork Head Chops with Vegetables

Prep time: 9 minutes | Cook time: 24 minutes | Serves 4

- 4 pork head chops
- 2 red tomatoes
- 1 large green pepper
- 4 mushrooms
- 1 onion
- 4 slices cheese
- Salt to taste
- Ground pepper to taste
- Extra-virgin olive oil

1. Put the chops on a plate and season with salt and pepper.
2. Put 2 of the chops in the air fryer basket. Add the tomato slices, cheese slices, pepper slices, onion slices, and mushroom slices. Add some threads of oil. Cook at 375°F for 24 minutes.
3. Check that the meat is well made and remove it.
4. Repeat the same operation with the other 2 pork chops.

PER SERVING

Calories: 105.3 | Fat: 3g | Carbs: 0g | Protein: 21.4g

Meat Pizza

Prep time: 10 minutes | Cook time: 15 minutes | Serves 2

- 8 oz ground beef
- 1 tablespoon marinara sauce
- ½ teaspoon dried oregano
- 1/3 cup Cheddar cheese, shredded
- ½ teaspoon coconut oil, melted
- ¼ teaspoon dried cilantro

1. Mix ground beef with dried cilantro and dried oregano.
2. Brush the air fryer basket with coconut oil.
3. Make 2 flat balls from the ground beef and put them in the air fryer basket.
4. Top them with marinara sauce and Cheddar cheese.
5. Cook the pizza at 375°F for 15 minutes.

PER SERVING

Calories: 304 | Fat: 14.7g | Fiber: 0.4g | Carbs: 1.6g | Protein: 39.3

Oregano Pork Chops

Prep time: 5 minutes | Cook time: 25 minutes | Serves 4

- 4 pork chops A pinch of salt and black pepper
- 2/3 cup cream cheese, soft
- ¼ teaspoon garlic powder
- ¼ teaspoon thyme, dried
- 1 tablespoon olive oil
- 1 tablespoon parsley, chopped

1. In a baking dish that fits your air fryer, mix all the ingredients, introduce the pan in the fryer and cook at 400 °F for 25 minutes.
2. Divide everything between plates and serve.

PER SERVING

Calories: 284| Fat: 14| Fiber: 4| Carbs: 6| Protein: 22

Beef Under Cabbage Blanket

Prep time: 10 minutes | Cook time: 50 minutes | Serves 4

- 2-pounds beef sirloin, diced
- 1 cup white cabbage, shredded
- ½ cup beef broth
- 1 teaspoon taco seasonings
- 1 teaspoon coconut oil
- 1 teaspoon salt

1. Mix beef sirloin with taco seasonings and salt.
2. Put the coconut oil in the air fryer basket. Add beef sirloin and beef broth.
3. Then top the beef with white cabbage.
4. Cook the meal at 360°F for 50 minutes.

PER SERVING

Calories: 440 | Fat: 15.5g | Fiber: 0.4g | Carbs: 1.1g | Protein: 69.6 g

Lamb Fritters

Prep time: 15 minutes | Cook time: 20 minutes | Serves 8

- 1 teaspoon onion powder
- 1 teaspoon garlic powder
- ½ teaspoon ground coriander
- 1 teaspoon salt
- 2-pound lamb, minced
- ½ cup cauliflower, shredded
- Cooking spray

1. Spray the air fryer basket with cooking spray from inside.
2. Then mix onion powder with garlic powder, ground coriander, salt, lamb, and cauliflower.
3. Make the fritters from the beef mixture and put them in the air fryer.
4. Cook the fritters at 360°F for 10 minutes per side.

PER SERVING

Calories: 215 | Fat: 8.3g | Fiber: 0.2g | Carbs: 0.8g | Protein: 32.1 g

Beef Casserole

Prep time: 10 minutes | Cook time: 40 minutes | Serves 4

- 2 oz Provolone cheese, grated
- 1 teaspoon coconut oil, softened
- 1 teaspoon dried cilantro
- 2-pounds ground beef
- 1 jalapeno pepper, sliced
- 1 teaspoon chili powder
- ¼ cup beef broth

1. Grease the air fryer basket with coconut oil.
2. Then mix ground beef with dried cilantro, jalapeno pepper, and chili powder.
3. Put the mixture in the air fryer basket.
4. Add beef broth and Provolone cheese.
5. Cook the casserole at 360°F for 40 minutes.

PER SERVING

Calories: 486 | Fat: 19.3g | Fiber: 0.3g | Carbs: 0.9g | Protein: 72.9 g

The Low-Carb Air Fryer Cookbook

Rosemary Lamb

Prep time: 5 minutes | Cook time: 30 minutes | Serves 4

- 1 tablespoon olive oil
- 2 garlic clove, minced
- 1 tablespoon rosemary, chopped
- ¼ cup keto tomato sauce
- 1 cup baby spinach
- 1 and ½ pounds lamb, cubed
- Salt and black pepper to the taste

1. Heat up a pan that fits the air fryer with the oil over medium heat, add the lamb and garlic and brown for 5 minutes.
2. Add the rest of the ingredients except the spinach, introduce the pan in the fryer and cook at 390 °F for 15 minutes, shaking the machine halfway.
3. Add the spinach, cook for 10 minutes more, divide between plates and serve for lunch.

PER SERVING
Calories: 257| Fat: 12| Fiber: 3| Carbs: 6| Protein: 14

Herbed Pork Skewers

Prep time: 10 minutes | Cook time: 20 minutes | Serves 4

- ½ pound pork shoulder, cubed
- ¼ teaspoon sweet paprika
- 1 tablespoon coconut oil, melted
- ¼ teaspoon cumin, ground
- ¼ cup olive oil
- ¼ cup green bell peppers, chopped
- 1 and ½ tablespoons lemon juice
- 1 tablespoon cilantro, chopped
- 2 tablespoons parsley, chopped
- 2 garlic cloves, minced Apinch of salt and black pepper

1. In a blender, combine the olive oil with bell peppers, lemon juice, cilantro, parsley, garlic, salt and pepper and pulse well.
2. Thread the meat onto the skewers, sprinkle cumin and paprika all over and rub with the coconut oil.
3. In a bowl mix the pork skewers with the herbed mix and rub well.
4. Place the skewers in your air fryer's basket, cook at 370 °F for 10 minutes on each side and serve as an appetizer.

PER SERVING
Calories: 249| Fat: 16| Fiber: 2| Carbs: 3| Protein: 17

Chili Tomato Pork

Prep time: 15 minutes | Cook time: 15 minutes | Serves 3

- 12 oz pork tenderloin
- 1 tablespoon grain mustard
- 1 tablespoon swerve
- 1 tablespoon keto tomato sauce
- 1 teaspoon chili pepper, grinded
- ¼ teaspoon garlic powder
- 1 tablespoon olive oil

1. In the mixing bowl mix up grain mustard, swerve, tomato sauce, chili pepper, garlic powder, and olive oil.
2. Rub the pork tenderloin with mustard mixture generously and leave for 5-10 minutes to marinate.
3. Meanwhile, preheat the air fryer to 370F.
4. Put the marinated pork tenderloin in the air fryer baking pan.
5. Then insert the baking pan in the preheated air fryer and cook the meat for 15 minutes.
6. Cool the cooked meat to the room temperature and slice it into the servings.

PER SERVING

Calories: 212| Fat: 9| Fiber: 0.2| Carbs: 6.4| Protein: 29.8

Beef, Lettuce and Cabbage Salad

Prep time: 5 minutes | Cook time: 25 minutes | Serves 4

- 1 pound beef, cubed
- ¼ cup coconut aminos
- 1 tablespoon coconut oil, melted
- 6 ounces iceberg lettuce, shredded
- 2 tablespoons cilantro, chopped
- 2 tablespoons chives, chopped
- 1 zucchini, shredded
- ½ green cabbage head, shredded
- 2 tablespoons almonds, sliced
- 1 tablespoon sesame seeds
- ½ tablespoon white vinegar A pinch of salt and black pepper

1. Heat up a pan that fits the air fryer with the oil over medium-high heat, add the meat and brown for 5 minutes.
2. Add the aminos, zucchini, cabbage, salt and pepper, toss, put the pan in the fryer and cook at 370 °F for 20 minutes.
3. Cool the mix down, transfer to a salad bowl, add the rest of the ingredients, toss well and serve.

PER SERVING

Calories: 270| Fat: 12| Fiber: 4| Carbs: 6| Protein: 16

The Low-Carb Air Fryer Cookbook

Masala Meatloaf

Prep time: 10 minutes | Cook time: 20 minutes | Serves 4

- 2 cups ground beef
- 1 large egg, beaten
- 2 spring onions, chopped
- 1 teaspoon garam masala
- ½ teaspoon ground ginger
- 1 teaspoon garlic powder
- ½ teaspoon salt
- ½ teaspoon ground turmeric
- ½ teaspoon cayenne pepper
- 1 teaspoon olive oil
- ¼ teaspoon ground nutmeg

1. In the mixing bowl mix up ground beef, egg, onion, garam masala, ground ginger, garlic powder, salt, ground turmeric, cayenne pepper, and ground nutmeg.
2. Stir the mass with the help of the spoon until homogenous.
3. Then brush the round air fryer pan with olive oil and place the ground beef mixture inside.
4. Press the meatloaf gently.
5. Place the pan with meatloaf in the air fryer and cook for 20 minutes at 365°F.

PER SERVING

Calories: 174| Fat: 10.8| Fiber: 0.8| Carbs: 3.7| Protein: 15.1

Beef Burger

Prep time: 10 minutes | Cook time: 15 minutes | Serves 3

- ½ teaspoon salt
- 1 teaspoon cayenne pepper
- 1 teaspoon minced ginger
- 1 teaspoon minced garlic
- 2 tablespoons chives, chopped
- 6 lettuce leaves
- 10 oz ground beef
- 1 tablespoon avocado oil
- 1 teaspoon gochujang

1. In the shallow bowl mix up gochujang, minced ginger, minced garlic, cayenne pepper, and salt.
2. Then mix up ground beef and churned spices mixture.
3. Add chives and stir the ground beef mass with the help of the fork until homogenous.
4. Preheat the air fryer to 365°F.
5. Then make 3 burgers from the ground beef mixture and put them in the air fryer.
6. Sprinkle the burgers with avocado oil and cook for 10 minutes at 365°F.
7. Then flip the burgers on another side and cook for 5 minutes more.

PER SERVING

Calories: 195| Fat: 11.7| Fiber: 1.1| Carbs: 3.4| Protein: 18.1

Chapter 5

Fish & Seafood

Shrimp and Spring Onions Stew

Prep time: 5 minutes | Cook time: 12 minutes | Serves 4

- 1 red bell pepper, chopped
- 14 ounces chicken stock
- 2 tablespoons keto tomato sauce
- 3 spring onions, chopped
- 1 and ½ pounds shrimp, peeled and deveined
- Salt and black pepper to the taste
- 1 tablespoon olive oil

1. In your air fryer's pan greased with the oil, mix the shrimp and the other ingredients, toss, introduce the pan in the machine, and cook at 360 °F for 12 minutes, stirring halfway.
2. Divide into bowls and serve for lunch.

PER SERVING

Calories: 223| Fat: 12| Fiber: 2| Carbs: 5| Protein: 9

Crab Dip

Prep time: 5 minutes | Cook time: 20 minutes | Serves 4

- 8 ounces cream cheese, soft
- 1 tablespoon lemon juice
- 1 cup coconut cream
- 1 tablespoon lemon juice
- 1 bunch green onions, minced
- 1 pound artichoke hearts, drained and chopped
- 12 ounces jumbo crab meat
- A pinch of salt and black pepper
- 1 and ½ cups mozzarella, shredded

1. In a bowl, combine all the ingredients except half of the cheese and whisk them really well.
2. Transfer this to a pan that fits your air fryer, introduce in the machine and cook at 400 °F for 15 minutes.
3. Sprinkle the rest of the mozzarella on top and cook for 5 minutes more.
4. Divide the mix into bowls and serve as a party dip.

PER SERVING

Calories: 240| Fat: 8| Fiber: 2| Carbs: 4| Protein: 14

Tuna Stuffed Avocado

Prep time: 15 minutes | Cook time: 12 minutes | Serves 2

- 1 avocado, pitted, halved
- ½ pound smoked tuna, boneless and shredded
- 1 egg, beaten
- ½ teaspoon salt
- ½ teaspoon chili powder
- ½ teaspoon ground nutmeg
- 1 teaspoon dried parsley
- Cooking spray

1. Scoop ½ part of the avocado meat from the avocado to get the avocado boats.
2. Use the scooper for this step.
3. After this, in the mixing bowl mix up tuna and egg.
4. Shred the mixture with the help of the fork.
5. Add salt, chili powder, ground nutmeg, and dried parsley.
6. Stir the tuna mixture until homogenous.
7. Add the scooped avocado meat and mix up the mixture well.
8. Fill the avocado boats with tuna mixture.
9. Preheat the air fryer to 385F.
10. Arrange the tuna boats in the air fryer basket and cook them for 12 minutes.

PER SERVING

Calories: 400| Fat: 29| Fiber: 7.1| Carbs: 9.5| Protein: 27.4

Crab Buns

Prep time: 15 minutes | Cook time: 20 minutes | Serves 2

- 5 oz crab meat, chopped
- 2 eggs, beaten
- 2 tablespoons coconut flour
- ¼ teaspoon baking powder
- ½ teaspoon coconut aminos
- ½ teaspoon ground black pepper
- 1 tablespoon coconut oil, softened

1. In the mixing bowl, mix crab meat with eggs, coconut flour, baking powder, coconut aminos, ground black pepper, and coconut oil.
2. Knead the smooth dough and cut it into pieces.
3. Make the buns from the crab mixture and put them in the air fryer basket.
4. Cook the crab buns at 365°F for 20 minutes.

PER SERVING

Calories: 217 | Fat: 13.2g | Fiber: 3.2g | Carbs: 7.3g | Protein: 15.5 g

Crab Cake

Prep time: 10 minutes | Cook time: 15 minutes | Serves 2

- 8 ounces crab meat, wild-caught
- 2 tablespoons almond flour
- 1/4 cup red bell pepper, cored, chopped
- 2 green onion, chopped
- 1 teaspoon old bay seasoning
- 1 tablespoon Dijon mustard
- 2 tablespoons mayonnaise, reduced fat

1. Switch on the air fryer, insert fryer basket, grease it with olive oil, then shut with its lid, set the fryer at 370 °F, and preheat for 5 minutes.
2. Meanwhile, place all the ingredients in a bowl, stir until well combined and then shape the mixture into four patties.
3. When air fryer beeps, open its lid, transfer the crab patties onto a serving plate and serve with lemon wedges.

PER SERVING

Calories:123 | Fat:6g |Carbs: 5g | Protein: 12g

The Low-Carb Air Fryer Cookbook

Parmesan Garlic Crusted Salmon

Prep time: 5 minutes | Cook time: 15 minutes | Serves 2

- 1/4 cup whole-wheat breadcrumbs
- 4 cups salmon
- 1 tbsp. butter, melted
- 1/4 tsp. freshly ground black pepper
- 1/4 cup Parmesan cheese, grated
- 2 tsp. garlic, minced
- 1/2 tsp. Italian seasoning

1. Let the air fryer preheat to 400°F, spray the oil over the air fryer basket.
2. Pat the salmon dry.
3. In a bowl, mix Parmesan cheese, Italian seasoning, and breadcrumbs. In another pan, mix melted butter with garlic and add to the breadcrumbs mix. Mix well.
4. Add kosher salt and freshly ground black pepper to salmon. On top of every salmon piece, add the crust mix and press gently.
5. Let the air fryer preheat to 400°F and add salmon to it. Cook until done to your liking (about 15 minutes).
6. Serve hot with vegetable side dishes.

PER SERVING

Calories: 339.5 | Fat: 18.7g | Protein: 31.5g | Carbs: 7.1g | Sugars: 0.2g

Sardine Cakes

Prep time: 15 minutes | Cook time: 10 minutes | Serves 5

- 12 oz sardines, trimmed, cleaned
- ¼ cup coconut flour
- 1 egg, beaten
- 2 tablespoons flax meal
- 1 teaspoon ground black pepper
- 1 teaspoon salt
- Cooking spray

1. Chop the sardines roughly and put them in the bowl.
2. Add coconut flour, egg, flax meal, ground black pepper, and salt.
3. Mix up the mixture with the help of the fork.
4. Then make 5 cakes from the sardine mixture.
5. Preheat the air fryer to 390F.
6. Spray the air fryer basket with cooking spray and place the cakes inside.
7. Cook them for 5 minutes from each side.

PER SERVING

Calories: 1700 | Fat: 9.8 | Fiber: 1.2 | Carbs: 1.5 | Protein: 18.6

Lime Baked Salmon

Prep time: 22 minutes | Cook time: 12 minutes | Serves 2

- 2 (3 oz.) salmon fillets, skin removed
- 1/4 cup jalapeños, sliced and pickled
- 1/2 medium lime, juiced
- 2 tbsp. cilantro, chopped
- 1 tbsp. salted butter; melted.
- 1/2 tsp. garlic, finely minced
- 1 tsp. chili powder

1. Place the salmon fillets into a 6-inch round baking pan.
2. Brush each with butter and sprinkle with chili powder and garlic.
3. Place the jalapeño slices on top and around salmon.
4. Pour half of the lime juice over the salmon and cover with foil. Place pan into the air fryer basket.
5. Adjust the temperature to 370°F and set the timer for 12 minutes.
6. When fully cooked, salmon should flake easily with a fork and reach an internal temperature of at least 145°F.
7. To serve, spritz with the remaining lime juice and garnish with cilantro.

PER SERVING

Calories: 166.8 | Protein: 18.5g | Fiber: 7g | Fat: 8.7g | Carbs: 5.8g

Ginger Cod Mix

Prep time: 15 minutes | Cook time: 11 minutes | Serves 4

- 1-pound cod fillet
- 1 teaspoon minced ginger
- ½ teaspoon ground ginger
- 1 tablespoon avocado oil
- ½ teaspoon salt
- ½ teaspoon ground paprika
- ½ teaspoon dried thyme

1. Rub the cod fillet with minced ginger and sprinkle with avocado oil.
2. Leave the fish for 10 minutes to marinate.
3. Meanwhile, mix up ground ginger, salt, ground paprika, and thyme in the shallow bowl.
4. Rub the marinated cod with the spice mixture.
5. Preheat the air fryer to 390F.
6. Put the cod in the air fryer basket and cook it for 6 minutes.
7. After this, flip the fish on another side and cook for 5 minutes more.

PER SERVING

Calories: 98| Fat: 1.5| Fiber: 0.4| Carbs: 0.7| Protein: 20.4

Chili Sea Bass Mix

Prep time: 5 minutes | Cook time: 15 minutes | Serves 4

- 4 sea bass fillets, boneless
- 4 garlic cloves, minced
- Juice of 1 lime
- 1 cup veggie stock Apinch of salt and black pepper
- 1 tablespoon black peppercorns, crushed
- 1-inch ginger, grated
- 4 lemongrass, chopped
- 4 small chilies, minced
- 1 bunch coriander, chopped

1. In a blender, combine all the ingredients except the fish and pulse well.
2. Pour the mix in a pan that fits the air fryer, add the fish, toss, introduce in the fryer and cook at 380 °F for 15 minutes.
3. Divide between plates and serve.

PER SERVING

Calories: 271| Fat: 12| Fiber: 4| Carbs: 6| Protein: 12

The Low-Carb Air Fryer Cookbook

Seafood Salad

Prep time: 10 minutes | Cook time: 5 minutes | Serves 4

- ½ cup mozzarella, shredded
- 1 tablespoon apple cider vinegar
- 1 teaspoon white pepper
- 1 cup lettuce, chopped
- 1-pound shrimps, peeled
- 1 teaspoon avocado oil
- 1 teaspoon chili powder

1. Mix shrimps with white pepper and apple cider vinegar.
2. Cook the shrimps in the air fryer at 400F for 5 minutes.
3. Then put the shrimps in the salad bowl.
4. Add all remaining ingredients and shake the salad.

PER SERVING

Calories: 152 | Fat: 2.9g | Fiber: 0.5g | Carbs: 3.1g | Protein: 27 g

Grilled Salmon with Lemon

Prep time: 120 minutes | Cook time: 10 minutes | Serves 4

- Olive oil: 2 tablespoons
- 2 Salmon fillets
- Lemon juice
- Water: 1/3 cup
- Gluten-free light soy sauce: 1/3 cup
- Honey: 1/3 cup
- Scallion slices
- Cherry tomato
- Freshly ground black pepper, garlic powder, kosher salt to taste

1. Season salmon with pepper and salt
2. In a bowl, mix honey, soy sauce, lemon juice, water, oil. Add salmon in this marinade and let it rest for least two hours.
3. Let the air fryer preheat at 180°C
4. Put and cook the fish in the air fryer and for 8 minutes.
5. Move to a dish and top with scallion slices.

PER SERVING

Calories: 211 | Fat: 9g | Carbs: 4.9g | Protein: 15g

Stuffed Mackerel

Prep time: 15 minutes | Cook time: 20 minutes | Serves 5

- 1-pound mackerel, trimmed
- 1 bell pepper, chopped
- ½ cup spinach, chopped
- 1 tablespoon avocado oil
- 1 teaspoon ground black pepper
- 1 teaspoon keto tomato paste

1. In the mixing bowl, mix bell pepper with spinach, ground black pepper, and tomato paste.
2. Fill the mackerel with spinach mixture.
3. Then brush the fish with avocado oil and put it in the air fryer.
4. Cook the fish at 365°F for 20 minutes.

PER SERVING

Calories: 252 | Fat: 16.6g | Fiber: 0.7g | Carbs: 0.5g | Protein: 22.1 g

Thyme Catfish

Prep time:10 minutes |Cook time: 12 minutes |Serves 4

- 20 oz catfish fillet (4 oz each fillet)
- 2 eggs, beaten
- 1 teaspoon dried thyme
- ½ teaspoon salt
- 1 teaspoon apple cider vinegar
- 1 teaspoon avocado oil
- ¼ teaspoon cayenne pepper
- 1/3 cup coconut flour

1. Sprinkle the catfish fillets with dried thyme, salt, apple cider vinegar, cayenne pepper, and coconut flour.
2. Then sprinkle the fish fillets with avocado oil.
3. Preheat the air fryer to 385F.
4. Put the catfish fillets in the air fryer basket and cook them for 8 minutes.
5. Then flip the fish on another side and cook for 4 minutes more.

PER SERVING

Calories: 198| Fat: 10.7| Fiber: 4.2| Carbs: 6.5| Protein: 18.3

Cajun Shrimps

Prep time:10 minutes |Cook time: 6 minutes |Serves 4

- 8 oz shrimps, peeled
- 1 teaspoon Cajun spices
- 1 teaspoon cream cheese
- 1 egg, beaten
- ½ teaspoon salt
- 1 teaspoon avocado oil

1. Sprinkle the shrimps with Cajun spices and salt.
2. In the mixing bowl mix up cream cheese and egg, Dip every shrimp in the egg mixture.
3. Preheat the air fryer to 400F.
4. Place the shrimps in the air fryer and sprinkle with avocado oil.
5. Cook the popcorn shrimps for 6 minutes.
6. Shake them well after 3 minutes of cooking.

PER SERVING

Calories: 88| Fat: 2.5| Fiber: 0.1| Carbs: 1| Protein: 14.4

Squid Stuffed with Cauliflower Mix

Prep time:20 minutes |Cook time: 6 minutes |Serves 4

- 4 squid tubes, trimmed
- 1 teaspoon ground paprika
- ½ teaspoon ground turmeric
- ½ teaspoon garlic, diced
- ½ cup cauliflower, shredded
- 1 egg, beaten
- ½ teaspoon salt
- ½ teaspoon ground ginger
- Cooking spray

1. Clean the squid tubes if needed.
2. After this, in the mixing bowl mix up ground paprika, turmeric, garlic, shredded cauliflower, salt, and ground ginger.
3. Stir the mixture gently and add a beaten egg.
4. Secure the edges of the squid tubes with toothpicks.
5. Preheat the air fryer to 390F.
6. Place the stuffed squid tubes in the air fryer and spray with cooking spray.
7. Cook the meal for 6 minutes.

PER SERVING

Calories: 8.| Fat: 2.7| Fiber: 0.6| Carbs: 1.5| Protein: 13.8

The Low-Carb Air Fryer Cookbook

Lemon and Oregano Tilapia Mix

Prep time: 5 minutes | Cook time: 20 minutes | Serves 4

- 4 tilapia fillets, boneless and halved
- Salt and black pepper to the taste
- 1 cup roasted peppers, chopped
- ¼ cup keto tomato sauce
- 1 cup tomatoes, cubed
- 1 tablespoon lemon juice
- 2 tablespoons olive oil
- 1 teaspoon garlic powder
- 1 teaspoon oregano, dried

1. In a baking dish that fits your air fryer, mix the fish with all the other ingredients, toss, introduce in your air fryer and cook at 380 °F for 20 minutes.
2. Divide into bowls and serve.

PER SERVING

Calories: 250| Fat: 9| Fiber: 2| Carbs: 5| Protein: 14

Crispy Fish Sandwiches

Prep time: 10 minutes | Cook time: 10 minutes | Serves 2

- 2 fillets Cod
- 2 tablespoons All-purpose flour
- 1/4 teaspoon Pepper
- 1 tablespoon Lemon juice
- 1/4 teaspoon Salt
- 1/2 teaspoon Garlic powder
- 1 egg
- 1/2 tablespoon Mayo
- 1/2 cup Whole wheat breadcrumbs

1. In a bowl, add salt, flour, pepper, and garlic powder.
2. In a separate bowl, add lemon juice, mayo, and egg.
3. In another bowl, add the breadcrumbs.
4. Coat the fish in flour, then in egg, then in breadcrumbs.
5. with cooking oil, spray the basket and put the fish in the basket. Also, spray the fish with cooking oil.
6. Cook at 400 F for ten minutes. This fish is soft, be careful if you flip.

PER SERVING

Calories: 218 | Fat: 12g | Carbs: 7g | Protein: 22g

Air Fryer Shrimp Scampi

Prep time: 5 minutes | Cook time: 7 minutes | Serves 2

- 4 cups raw shrimp
- 1 tbsp. lemon juice
- 1/2 tsp. fresh basil, chopped
- 2 tsp. red pepper flakes
- 4 tbsp. butter
- 1/4 cup chives, chopped
- 1 tbsp. chicken stock
- 1 tbsp. garlic, minced

1. Let the air fryer preheat with a metal pan to 330°F.
2. In the hot pan, add the garlic, red pepper flakes, and half of the butter. Let it cook for 2 minutes. Add the butter, shrimp, chicken stock, minced garlic, chives, lemon juice, basil to the pan. Let it cook for 5 minutes. Bathe the shrimp in melted butter.
3. Take it out from the air fryer and let it rest for 1 minute. Let it cook for 2 minutes. Add the fresh basil leaves and chives and serve.

PER SERVING

Calories: 286.5 | Fat: 5.1g | Protein: 18.5g | Carbs: 6.3g | Sugar: 2.2g

Chapter 6

Side Dishes and Snacks

Eggplant Lasagna

Prep time: 20 minutes | Cook time: 30 minutes | Serves 6

- 2 medium eggplants
- ½ cup keto tomato sauce
- 1 cup Cheddar cheese, shredded
- ½ cup Mozzarella cheese, shredded
- 1 cup ground pork
- 1 teaspoon Italian seasonings
- 1 teaspoon sesame oil

1. Slice the eggplants into the long slices.
2. Then brush the air fryer pan with sesame oil.
3. In the mixing bowl mix up ground pork and Italian seasonings.
4. Then make the layer from the sliced eggplants in the air fryer pan.
5. Top it with a small amount of ground pork and mozzarella cheese.
6. Then sprinkle mozzarella with the tomato sauce Place the second eggplant layer over the sauce and repeat all the steps again.
7. Cover the last layer with remaining eggplant and top with Cheddar cheese.
8. Cover the lasagna with foil and place it in the air fryer.
9. Cook the meal for 20 minutes at 365°F.
10. Then remove the foil from the lasagna and cook it for 10 minutes more.
11. Let the cooked lasagna cool for 10 minutes before serving.

PER SERVING

Calories: 260| Fat: 18.7| Fiber: 0.8| Carbs: 3| Protein: 19.6

Parmesan Cauliflower Risotto

Prep time: 10 minutes | Cook time: 18 minutes | Serves 4

- 1 cup cauliflower, shredded
- 4 oz cremini mushrooms, sliced
- 2 oz Parmesan, grated
- 1 teaspoon ground black pepper
- 1 tablespoon heavy cream
- 3 spring onions, diced
- 1 tablespoon olive oil
- ½ teaspoon Italian seasonings

1. Preheat the air fryer to 400f.
2. Then sprinkle the air fryer basket with olive oil.
3. Place the mushrooms inside and sprinkle them with ground black pepper.
4. Cook them at 400F for 4 minutes.
5. Then stir them well and add the spring onion.
6. Cook the vegetables for 4 minutes more.
7. Then shake them well and sprinkle with garlic powder and Italian seasonings.
8. Mix up well and transfer in the air fryer mold.
9. Add heavy cream and shredded cauliflower.
10. Then add parmesan and mix up.
11. Place the mold in the air fryer and cook for 10 minutes at 375°F.
12. Then mix up risotto and transfer in the serving plates.

PER SERVING

Calories: 112 fat 8.2| Fiber: 1.3| Carbs: 5| Protein: 6.2

Mushroom Cakes

Prep time: 10 minutes | Cook time: 8 minutes | Serves 4

- 9 oz mushrooms, finely chopped
- ¼ cup coconut flour
- 1 teaspoon salt
- 1 egg, beaten
- 3 oz Cheddar cheese, shredded
- 1 teaspoon dried parsley
- ½ teaspoon ground black pepper
- 1 teaspoon sesame oil
- 1 oz spring onion, chopped

1. In the mixing bowl mix up chopped mushrooms, coconut flour, salt, egg, dried parsley, ground black pepper, and minced onion.
2. Stir the mixture until smooth and add Cheddar cheese.
3. Stir it with the help of the fork, Preheat the air fryer to 385F.
4. Line the air fryer pan with baking paper.
5. with the help of the spoon make the medium size patties and put them in the pan.
6. Sprinkle the patties with sesame oil and cook for 4 minutes from each side.

PER SERVING

Calories: 164| Fat: 10.7| Fiber: 3.9| Carbs: 7.8| Protein: 10.3

Pork Minis

Prep time: 10 minutes | Cook time: 15 minutes | Serves 4

- 1 cup ground pork
- 1 teaspoon Italian seasonings
- ¼ cup Cheddar cheese, shredded
- 1 teaspoon tomato paste
- ½ teaspoon coconut oil

1. In the mixing bowl, mix ground pork with Italian seasonings, Cheddar cheese, and tomato paste.
2. Then make the minis from the mixture.
3. Grease the air fryer basket with coconut oil and put the pork minis inside.
4. Cook them for 15 minutes at 375°F.

PER SERVING

Calories: 157 | Fat: 6.2g | Fiber: 0.1g | Carbs: 0.5g | Protein: 23.6 g

Air Fryer Buffalo Cauliflower

Prep time: 5 minutes | Cook time: 15 minutes | Serves 4

- Homemade buffalo sauce: 1/2 cup
- One head of cauliflower, cut bite-size pieces
- Butter melted: 1 tablespoon
- Olive oil
- Kosher salt & pepper, to taste

1. Spray cooking oil on the air fryer basket.
2. In a bowl, add melted butter, buffalo sauce, pepper, and salt. Mix well.
3. Put the cauliflower bits in the air fryer and spray the olive oil over it. Let it cook at 400 F for 7 minutes.
4. Remove the cauliflower from the air fryer and add it to the sauce. Coat the cauliflower well.
5. Put the sauce coated cauliflower back into the air fryer.
6. Cook at 400 F, for 7-8 minutes. Take out from the air fryer and serve with dipping sauce.

PER SERVING

Calories: 100.8 | Carbs: 3.7g | Protein: 3.5g | Fat: 6.5g

The Low-Carb Air Fryer Cookbook

Parm Squash

Prep time:10 minutes |Cook time: 25 minutes |Serves 4

- 1 medium spaghetti squash
- 2 oz Mozzarella, shredded
- 1 oz Parmesan, shredded
- 1 teaspoon avocado oil
- ½ teaspoon dried oregano
- ½ teaspoon dried cilantro
- ½ teaspoon ground nutmeg
- 2 teaspoons butter

1. Cut the spaghetti squash into halves and remove the seeds.
2. Then sprinkle it with avocado oil, dried oregano, dried cilantro, and ground nutmeg.
3. Put 1 teaspoon of butter in every spaghetti squash half and transfer the vegetables in the air fryer.
4. Cook them for 15 minutes at 365°F.
5. After this, fill the squash with Mozzarella and Parmesan and cook for 10 minutes more at the same temperature.

PER SERVING

Calories: 91| Fat: 6.3| Fiber: 0.2| Carbs: 2.8| Protein: 6.5

Seafood Balls

Prep time: 15 minutes | Cook time: 15 minutes | Serves 4

- 1-pound salmon fillet, minced
- 1 egg, beaten
- 3 tablespoons coconut, shredded
- ½ cup almond flour
- 1 tablespoon avocado oil
- 1 teaspoon dried basil

1. In the mixing bowl, mix minced salmon fillet, egg, coconut, almond flour, and dried basil.
2. Make the balls from the fish mixture and put them in the air fryer basket.
3. Sprinkle the balls with avocado oil and cook at 365°F for 15 minutes.

PER SERVING

Calories: 268 | Fat: 16.4g | Fiber: 2g | Carbs: 3.9g | Protein: 26.6 g

Pull-apart Bread with Garlic Oil

Prep time: 10 minutes | Cook time:10 minutes |Serves 2

- 1 large vegan bread loaf
- 2 tablespoons garlic puree
- 2 tablespoons nutritional yeast
- 2 tablespoons olive oil
- 2 teaspoons chives
- salt and pepper to taste

1. Preheat the air fryer to 357°F.
2. Slice the bread loaf making sure that you don't slice through the bread.
3. In a mixing bowl, combine the olive oil, garlic puree, and nutritional yeast.
4. Pour over the mixture on top of the slices you made on the bread.
5. Place inside the air fryer and cook for 10 minutes or until the garlic is thoroughly cooked.

PER SERVING

Calories:51 | Fat:6g |Carbs: 1g | Protein: 1g

Portobello Patties

Prep time: 10 minutes | Cook time: 8 minutes | Serves 4

- 10 oz Portobello mushrooms, diced
- 1 egg, beaten
- 3 oz Monterey Jack cheese, shredded
- 1 teaspoon dried cilantro
- ½ teaspoon white pepper
- 1 teaspoon avocado oil
- 2 tablespoons coconut flour

1. Mix mushrooms with egg, Monterey Jack cheese, cilantro, white pepper, and coconut flour.
2. Make the patties from the mushroom mixture.
3. Then brush the air fryer basket with avocado oil and put the patties inside.
4. Cook them at 375°F for 4 minutes per side.

PER SERVING

Calories: 145 | Fat: 8.6g | Fiber: 3.7g | Carbs: 7.6g | Protein: 10.5 g

Cauliflower Bites

Prep time: 15 minutes | Cook time: 4 minutes | Serves 2

- 1 egg
- 1 cup cauliflower, shredded
- 1 teaspoon chives, chopped
- 1 tablespoon almond flour
- ¼ teaspoon salt
- 1 teaspoon ground turmeric
- 2 oz Pecorino cheese, grated
- Cooking spray

1. Crack the egg in the bowl and whisk it.
2. Add shredded cauliflower, chives, almond flour, and salt.
3. Mix up the mixture until it is homogenous.
4. Then add Pecorino cheese and turmeric, and stir it until smooth.
5. Make the small balls and press them gently with the help of the fingertips in the shape of nuggets.
6. Preheat the air fryer to 395F.
7. Place the cauli nuggets in the air fryer basket and spray them with cooking spray.
8. Cook the nuggets for 2 minutes from each side.
9. Cook the nuggets for 2 extra minutes for a saturated golden color.

PER SERVING

Calories: 211| Fat: 15.4| Fiber: 1.9| Carbs: 4.3| Protein: 16

Keto Granola

Prep time: 10 minutes | Cook time: 12 minutes | Serves 4

- 1 teaspoon monk fruit
- 2 teaspoons coconut oil
- 3 pecans, chopped
- 1 teaspoon pumpkin pie spices
- 1 tablespoon coconut shred
- 3 oz almonds, chopped
- 1 tablespoon flax seeds

1. In the mixing bowl, mix all ingredients from the list above.
2. Make the small balls from the mixture and put them in the air fryer.
3. Cook the granola for 6 minutes per side at 365°F.
4. Cool the cooked granola.

PER SERVING

Calories: 239 | Fat: 22.3g | Fiber: 4.6g | Carbs: 7.4g | Protein: 6 g

Potato Filled Bread Rolls

Prep time: 10 minutes | Cook time:25 minutes |Serves 4

- 5 large potatoes, boiled and mashed
- 1/2 tsp turmeric
- 2 green chilies, deseeded and chopped
- 1 medium onion, finely chopped
- 1/2 tsp mustard seeds
- 1 tbsp olive oil
- 2 sprigs curry leaf
- Salt to taste

1. Preheat air fryer to 350 F.
2. Combine olive oil, onion, curry leaves, and mustard seed in a baking dish.
3. Add in the air fryer basket and cook for 5 minutes. Mix the onion mixture with the mashed potatoes, chilies, turmeric, and salt.
4. Divide the mixture into 8 equal pieces. Trim the sides of the bread, and wet with some water. Make sure to get rid of the excess water.
5. Take one wet bread slice in your palm and place one of the potato pieces in the center.
6. Roll the bread over the filling, sealing the edges. Place the rolls onto a prepared baking dish, and air fry for 12 minutes.

PER SERVING

Calories:93 | Fat:1g |Carbs: 16g | Protein: 4g

Kale & Celery Crackers

Prep time: 10 minutes | Cook time: 20 minutes | Serves 6

- 1 cups flax seed, ground
- 1 cups flax seed, soaked overnight and drained
- 2 bunches kale, chopped
- 1 bunch basil, chopped
- ½ bunch celery, chopped
- 2 garlic cloves, minced
- 1/3 cup olive oil

1. Mix the ground flaxseed with the basil, kale, celery, and garlic in your food processor and mix well.
2. Add the oil and soaked flaxseed, then mix again.
3. Scatter in the pan of your air fryer, break into medium crackers and cook for 20 minutes at 380 °F.

PER SERVING

Calories: 142.7 | Fat: 1g | Fiber: 2g | Carbs: 7.8g | Protein: 4.5g

Spinach Mash

Prep time:10 minutes |Cook time: 13 minutes |Serves 4

- 3 cups spinach, chopped
- ½ cup Mozzarella, shredded
- 4 bacon slices, chopped
- 1 teaspoon butter
- 1 cup heavy cream
- ½ teaspoon salt
- ½ jalapeno pepper, chopped

1. Place the bacon in the air fryer and cook it for 8 minutes at 400F.
2. Stir it from time to time with the help of the spatula.
3. After this, put the cooked bacon in the air fryer casserole mold.
4. Add heavy cream spinach, jalapeno pepper, salt, butter, and Mozzarella.
5. Stir it gently.
6. Cook the mash for 5 minutes at 400F.
7. Then stir the spinach mash carefully with the help of the spoon.

PER SERVING

Calories: 230| Fat: 20.7| Fiber: 0.6| Carbs: 2.2| Protein: 9.3

Cream Cheese Zucchini

Prep time: 5 minutes | Cook time: 15 minutes | Serves 4

- 1 pound zucchinis, cut into wedges
- 1 cup cream cheese, soft
- 1 green onion, sliced
- 1 teaspoon garlic powder
- 2 tablespoons basil, chopped A pinch of salt and black pepper
- 1 tablespoon butter, melted

1. In a pan that fits your air fryer, mix the zucchinis with all the other ingredients, toss, introduce in the air fryer and cook at 370 °F for 15 minutes.
2. Divide between plates and serve as a side dish.

PER SERVING

Calories: 129| Fat: 6| Fiber: 2| Carbs: 5| Protein: 8

Almond Brussels Sprouts

Prep time: 10 minutes | Cook time: 15 minutes | Serves 4

- 8 oz Brussels sprouts
- 2 tablespoons almonds, grinded
- 1 teaspoon coconut flakes
- 2 egg whites
- ½ teaspoon salt
- ½ teaspoon white pepper
- Cooking spray

1. Whisk the egg whites and add salt and white pepper.
2. Then cut the Brussels sprouts into halves and put the egg white mixture.
3. Shake the vegetables well and then coat in the grinded almonds and coconut flakes.
4. Preheat the air fryer to 380F.
5. Place the Brussels sprouts in the air fryer basket and cook them for 15 minutes.
6. Shake the vegetables after 8 minutes of cooking.

PER SERVING

Calories: 52| Fat: 1.9| Fiber: 2.6| Carbs: 6.1| Protein: 4.4

Fried Broccoli From India

Prep time: 10 minutes | Cook time: 15 minutes | Serves 6

- 1/4 teaspoon turmeric powder
- 1/2 pounds broccoli, cut into florets
- 1 tablespoon almond flour
- 1 teaspoon garam masala
- 2 tablespoons coconut milk
- Salt and pepper to taste

1. Preheat the air fryer for 5 minutes.
2. In a bowl, combine all ingredients until the broccoli florets are coated with the other ingredients.
3. Place in a fryer basket and cook for 15 minutes until crispy.

PER SERVING

Calories: 114 | Fat: 5g | Carbs: 14g | Protein: 6g

Sweet Potato Cauliflower Patties

Prep time: 20 minutes | Cook time: 20 minutes | Serves 7

- 1 green onion, chopped
- 1 large sweet potato, peeled
- 1 tsp. garlic, minced
- 1 cup cilantro leaves
- 2 cup cauliflower florets
- 1/4 tsp. ground black pepper
- 1/4 tsp. salt
- 1/4 cup sunflower seeds
- 1/4 tsp. cumin
- 1/4 cup ground flaxseed
- 1/2 tsp. red chili powder
- 2 tbsp. ranch seasoning mix
- 2 tbsp. arrowroot starch

1. Cut peeled sweet potato into small pieces, then place them in a food processor and pulse until pieces are broken up.
2. Then add the garlic, cauliflower florets, onion, and pulse; add the remaining ingredients and pulse more until well combined.
3. Tip the mixture into a bowl, shape it into 7 1 1/2-inch thick patties, each about 1/4 cup, then place them on a baking sheet and freeze for 10 minutes.
4. Switch on the air fryer, insert the fryer basket, and grease it with olive oil; close the lid, set the fryer at 400°F, and preheat for 10 minutes.
5. Open the fryer, add patties to it in a single layer, and cook for 20 minutes; flipping the patties halfway through the frying.
6. When the air fryer beeps, open the lid, transfer the patties onto a serving plate, and keep them warm.
7. Prepare the continuing patties in the same way and serve.

PER SERVING

Calories: 84.5 | Carbs: 8.7g | Fat: 2.8g | Protein: 3.2g | Fiber: 3.5g

Almond Broccoli Rice

Prep time: 10 minutes | Cook time: 8 minutes | Serves 4

- 2 cup broccoli, shredded
- ½ teaspoon apple cider vinegar
- ¼ teaspoon salt
- 1 tablespoon cream cheese
- ½ teaspoon pumpkin seeds, crushed
- 1 tablespoon organic almond milk
- 1 teaspoon butter, melted

1. In the bowl mix up butter, broccoli, apple cider vinegar, salt, and pumpkin seeds.
2. Transfer the mixture in the baking pan for the air fryer.
3. Add almond milk and mix up the vegetable mixture until homogenous.
4. Cover it with the foil.
5. Preheat the air fryer to 375°F.
6. Then remove the pan from the air fryer and add cream cheese.
7. Stir the cooked broccoli rice well.

PER SERVING

Calories: 43 | Fat: 3 | Fiber: 1.3 | Carbs: 3.4 | Protein: 1.7

Chapter 7

Vegan & Vegetarian

Veggie Pizza

Prep time: 10 minutes | Cook time: 15 minutes | Serves 4

- 8 bacon slices
- ¼ cup black olives, sliced
- ¼ cup scallions, sliced
- 1 green bell pepper, sliced
- 1 cup Mozzarella, shredded
- 1 tablespoon keto tomato sauce
- ½ teaspoon dried basil
- ½ teaspoon sesame oil

1. Line the air fryer pan with baking paper.
2. Then make the layer of the sliced bacon in the pan and sprinkle gently with sesame oil.
3. Preheat the air fryer to 400F.
4. Place the pan with the bacon in the air fryer basket and cook it for 9 minutes at 400F.
5. After this, sprinkle the bacon with keto tomato sauce and top with Mozzarella.
6. Then add bell pepper, spring onions, and black olives.
7. Sprinkle the pizza with dried basil and cook for 6 minutes at 400F.

PER SERVING

Calories: 255| Fat: 18.8| Fiber: 0.9| Carbs: 4.5| Protein: 16.5

Mediterranean Vegetable Skewers

Prep time: 30 minutes | Cook time: 13 minutes | Serves 4

- 2 medium-sized zucchinis, cut into 1-inch pieces
- 2 red bell peppers, cut into 1-inch pieces
- 1 green bell pepper, cut into 1-inch pieces
- 1 red onion, cut into 1-inch pieces
- 2 tablespoons olive oil
- Sea salt, to taste
- 1/2 teaspoon black pepper, preferably freshly cracked
- 1/2 teaspoon red pepper flakes

1. Thread the vegetables on skewers; drizzle olive oil all over the vegetable skewers; sprinkle with spices.
2. Cook in the preheated Air Fryer at 400 °F for 13 minutes. Serve warm.

PER SERVING

Calories: 137.6 | Fat: 9.6g | Carbs: 9.5g | Protein: 2.8g | Sugars: 6.2g

Smoked Tempeh

Prep time: 10 minutes | Cook time: 6 minutes | Serves 2

- 1 cup tempeh
- 1 teaspoon apple cider vinegar
- 1 teaspoon sesame oil
- ½ teaspoon garlic powder
- 1 teaspoon liquid smoke
- 1 teaspoon butter, melted

1. In the shallow bowl mix up melted butter, liquid smoke, garlic powder, sesame oil, and apple cider vinegar.
2. Cut the tempeh into halves and brush with apple cider vinegar mixture from both sides.
3. After this, preheat the air fryer to 400F.
4. Put the tempeh in the air fryer and cook it for 3 minutes from each side or until it is light brown.
5. Transfer the cooked tempeh to the serving plate.
6. Vegan Reuben is cooked.

PER SERVING

Calories: 200| Fat: 13.2| Fiber: 0.1| Carbs: 8.3| Protein: 15.5

Fried Pickles

Prep time: 20 minutes | Cook time: 10 minutes | Serves 2

- 1 egg, whisked
- 2 tablespoons of buttermilk
- 1/2 cup of fresh breadcrumbs
- 1/4 cup of Romano cheese, grated
- 1/2 teaspoon of onion powder
- 1/2 teaspoon of garlic powder
- 1 ½ cups of dill pickle chips, pressed dry with kitchen towels

Mayo Sauce:
- 1/4 cup of mayonnaise
- 1/2 tablespoon of mustard
- 1/2 teaspoon of molasses
- 1 tablespoon of ketchup
- 1/4 teaspoon of ground black pepper

1. In a shallow bowl, whisk the egg with buttermilk.
2. In another bowl, mix the onion powder, cheese, breadcrumbs, and garlic powder.
3. Dip the pickle chips in the egg mixture, then, dredge with the mixture.
4. Cook in the preheated Air Fryer at 400°F for 5 minutes; shake the basket and cook for 5 minutes more.
5. Meanwhile, mix all the sauce ingredients until well combined. Serve the fried pickles with the mayo sauce for dipping.

PER SERVING

Calories: 341.5 | Fat: 28.1g | Carbs: 12.2g | Protein: 9.8g | Sugars: 4.2g

Eggplant Dip

Prep time: 10 minutes | Cook time: 15 minutes | Serves 4

- 1 eggplant, peeled
- 1 garlic clove, peeled
- 1 tablespoon sesame oil
- ¼ teaspoon ginger, grated
- 1 chili pepper, minced
- ½ tablespoon spring onions, chopped
- ½ teaspoon chili powder
- ¼ teaspoon ground coriander
- ¼ teaspoon turmeric
- ½ teaspoon fresh cilantro, chopped

1. Chop the eggplant into the cubes and put it in the air fryer.
2. Add garlic and cook the vegetables at 400F for 15 minutes.
3. Shake the vegetables every 5 minutes.
4. After this, transfer the soft eggplants and garlic in the bowl and mash them with the help of the fork.
5. Add sesame oil, ginger, minced chili pepper, onion, chili powder, ground coriander, and turmeric.
6. Stir the mixture until homogenous and top with cilantro.

PER SERVING

Calories: 63| Fat: 3.7| Fiber: 4.3| Carbs: 7.5| Protein: 1.3

Vegetarian Hash Browns

Prep time: 10 minutes | Cook time: 19 minutes | Serves 8

- 4 large potatoes, peeled, shredded
- 1 teaspoon onion powder
- 1 teaspoon garlic powder
- 2 teaspoons chili flakes
- salt and pepper to taste
- 2 tablespoons corn flour
- 2 teaspoons olive oil
- cooking spray as needed

1. Add potatoes to a bowl of cold water and leave them to soak for a few minutes then drain them and repeat. Add a teaspoon of olive oil into skillet and cook potatoes over medium heat for 4-minutes.
2. Place potatoes on plate to cool once they are cooked. In a large mixing bowl, add flour, potatoes, salt, pepper and other seasonings and combine well.
3. Place bowl in fridge for 20-minutes. Preheat your air fryer to 350°F. Remove hash browns from fridge and cut into size pieces you desire. Spray the wire basket of your air fryer with some oil, add the hash browns and fry them for 15-minutes. Halfway through flip them to help cook them all over. Serve hot!

PER SERVING

Calories: 242 | Total Fat: 13.1g | Carbs: 9.6g | Protein: 14.2g

Feta & Mushroom Frittata

Prep time: 10 minutes | Cook time: 30 minutes | Serves 4

- 1 red onion, thinly sliced
- 4 cups button mushrooms, thinly sliced
- salt to taste
- 6 tablespoons feta cheese, crumbled
- 6 medium eggs
- non-stick cooking spray
- 2 tablespoons olive oil

1. Sauté the onion and mushrooms in olive oil over medium heat until the vegetables are tender. Remove the vegetables from pan and drain on a paper towel-lined plate. In a mixing bowl, whisk eggs and salt.
2. Coat all sides of baking dish with cooking spray. Preheat your air fryer to 325°F. Pour the beaten eggs into prepared baking dish and scatter the sautéed vegetables and crumble feta on top. Bake in the air fryer for 30-minutes. Allow to cool slightly and serve!

PER SERVING

Calories: 226 | Total Fat: 9.3g | Carbs: 8.7g | Protein: 12.6g

Sweet Potato Fritters

Prep time: 6–7 minutes | Cook time: 4 minutes | Serves 4

- 1 can sweet potato puree, 15 oz.
- ½ tsp. minced garlic
- ½ cup frozen spinach, thawed, finely chopped, and drained well
- 1 large leek, minced
- 1 serving flax egg
- ¼ cup almond flour
- ¼ tsp. sweet paprika flakes
- 1 tsp. kosher salt
- ½ tsp. ground white pepper

1. Heat the Air Fryer to 330°F.
2. Place all ingredients in a bowl and mix all well. Divide into 16 balls and flatten each to the only an-inch-thick patty.
3. Place patties in the Air Fryer basket and cook for two minutes at 330°F. Flip and cook for 2 more minutes.
4. If needed, cook in batches.

PER SERVING

Calories: 231.5 | Fat: 7.5g | Carbs: 5.8g | Protein: 12.8g

Okra Salad

Prep time: 10 minutes | Cook time: 6 minutes | Serves 2

- 6 oz okra, sliced
- 3 oz green beans, chopped
- 1 cup arugula, chopped
- 1 teaspoon lemon juice
- 1 teaspoon olive oil
- ½ teaspoon salt
- 2 eggs, beaten
- 1 tablespoon coconut flakes
- Cooking spray

1. In the mixing bowl mix up sliced okra and green beans.
2. Add cooking spray and salt and mix up the mixture well.
3. Then add beaten eggs and shake it.
4. Preheat the air fryer to 400F.
5. Put the vegetable mixture in the air fryer and cook it for 6 minutes.
6. Shake the mixture after 3 minutes of cooking.
7. After this, mix up cooked vegetables with arugula, lemon juice, and sprinkle with olive oil.
8. Shake the salad.

PER SERVING

Calories: 142 | Fat: 7.8 | Fiber: 4.6 | Carbs: 10.5 | Protein: 8.3

Cheesy Rutabaga

Prep time: 15 minutes | Cook time: 8 minutes | Serves 2

- 6 oz rutabaga, chopped
- 2 oz Jarlsberg cheese, grated
- 1 tablespoon butter
- ½ teaspoon dried parsley
- ½ teaspoon salt
- ½ teaspoon minced garlic
- 3 tablespoons heavy cream

1. In the mixing bowl mix up a rutabaga, dried parsley, salt, and minced garlic.
2. Then add heavy cream and mix up the vegetables well.
3. After this, preheat the air fryer to 375°F.
4. Put the rutabaga mixture in the air fryer and cook it for 6 minutes.
5. Then stir it well and top with grated cheese.
6. Cook the meal for 2 minutes more.
7. Transfer the cooked rutabaga in the plates and top with butter.

PER SERVING

Calories: 262 | Fat: 22.4 | Fiber: 2.2 | Carbs: 7.8 | Protein: 8.7

Mustard Cabbage

Prep time: 10 minutes | Cook time: 40 minutes | Serves 4

- 1-pound white cabbage
- 1 teaspoon mustard
- 1 teaspoon ground black pepper
- ½ teaspoon salt
- 3 tablespoons butter, melted
- ½ teaspoon ground paprika
- ½ teaspoon chili flakes
- 1 teaspoon dried thyme

1. In the mixing bowl mix up mustard, ground black pepper, salt, butter, ground paprika, chili flakes, and dried thyme.
2. Brush the cabbage with the mustard mixture generously and place it in the air fryer.
3. Cook the cabbage for 40 minutes at 365°F.
4. Then cool the cooked vegetable to the room temperature and slice into servings.

PER SERVING

Calories: 111| Fat: 9.1| Fiber: 3.3| Carbs: 7.5| Protein: 1.9

Mushroom, Onion and Feta Frittata

Prep time: 10 minutes | Cook time: 30 minutes | Serves 4

- 4 cups button mushrooms
- 1 red onion
- 2 tablespoons olive oil
- 6 tablespoons feta cheese, crumbled
- pinch of salt
- 6 eggs
- cooking spray

1. Peel and slice the red onion into ¼ inch thin slices. Clean the button mushrooms, then cut them into ¼ inch thin slices. Add olive oil to pan and sauté mushrooms over medium heat until tender.
2. Remove from heat and pan so that they can cool. Preheat your air fryer to 330°F. Add cracked eggs into a bowl, and whisk them, adding a pinch of salt. Coat an 8-inch heat resistant baking dish with cooking spray. Add the eggs into the baking dish, then onion and mushroom mixture, and then add feta cheese.
3. Place the baking dish into air fryer for 30-minutes and serve warm.

PER SERVING

Calories: 246 | Total Fat: 12.3g | Carbs: 9.2g | Protein: 10.3g

Greens Salad

Prep time: 15 minutes | Cook time: 10 minutes | Serves 4

- 1 cup asparagus, chopped, cooked
- 6 oz Swiss chard, chopped
- 1 teaspoon garlic powder
- 1 tablespoon almonds, chopped
- 1 tablespoon apple cider vinegar
- 8 oz chicken fillet
- 1 teaspoon avocado oil
- 1 teaspoon olive oil

1. Chop the chicken fillet roughly and mix it with olive oil, garlic powder, and apple cider vinegar.
2. Cook the chicken in the air fryer at 375°F for 10 minutes.
3. Then mix cooked chicken with remaining ingredients and shake well.

PER SERVING

Calories: 146 | Fat: 6.4g | Fiber: 1.7g | Carbs: 3.8g | Protein: 18.4

The Low-Carb Air Fryer Cookbook

Buffalo Cauliflower Wings

Prep time: 5 minutes | Cook time: 15 minutes | Serves 6

- 1 tablespoon of almond flour
- 1 medium head of cauliflower
- 1 ½ teaspoon of salt
- 4 tablespoons of hot sauce
- 1 tablespoon of olive oil

1. Switch on the Air Fryer, insert fryer basket, grease it with olive oil, then shut with its lid, set the fryer to 400°F, and preheat for 5 minutes.
2. Meanwhile, cut cauliflower into bite-size florets and set aside.
3. Place flour in a large bowl, whisk in salt, oil, and hot sauce until combined, add cauliflower florets and toss until combined.
4. When the Air Fryer beeps, open its lid, transfer cauliflower florets onto a serving plate and keep warm.
5. Cook the remaining cauliflower florets the same way and serve.

PER SERVING

Calories: 47.5 | Carbs: 0.6g | Fat: 3.5g | Protein: 1.6g | Fiber: 0.5g

Spicy Glazed Carrots

Prep time: 20 minutes | Cook time: 15 minutes | Serves 3

- 1 pound carrots, cut into matchsticks
- 2 tablespoons of peanut oil
- 1 tablespoon of agave syrup
- 1 jalapeño, seeded and minced
- 1/4 teaspoon of dill
- 1/2 teaspoon of basil
- Salt and white pepper to taste

1. Start by warming your Air Fryer to 380°F.
2. Toss all ingredients together and place them in the Air Fryer basket. Cook for 15 minutes, shaking the basket halfway through the Cooking Time.

PER SERVING

Calories: 161.5 | Fat: 9g | Carbs: 19.6g | Protein: 1.8g | Sugars: 12.8g

Spinach Tortillas

Prep time:15 minutes |Cook time: 10 minutes |Serves 2

- 1 cup spinach, chopped
- ½ cup coconut flour
- ½ teaspoon salt
- 1 egg, beaten
- 1 cup water, boiled, hot
- 1 teaspoon butter, softened

1. Put spinach in the bowl and add hot water.
2. Leave the greens in hot water for 5 minutes.
3. Then remove the spinach from the water and transfer in the blender.
4. Blend it until you get a smooth texture.
5. Put the blended spinach in the bowl and add coconut flour, salt, egg, and butter.
6. Knead the soft dough and cut it into small pieces.
7. Roll up every dough piece in the tortilla shape.
8. Preheat the air fryer to 400F.
9. Put the spinach tortilla in the air fryer and cook it for 2 minutes from each side.
10. Repeat the same steps with all remaining tortillas.

PER SERVING

Calories: 192| Fat: 9.2| Fiber: 12.3| Carbs: 18.7| Protein: 9.2

Cheese Stuffed Mushrooms

Prep time: 15 minutes | Cook time: 7 minutes | Serves 3

- 9 large button mushrooms, stems removed
- 1 tbsp. olive oil
- Salt and ground black pepper, to taste
- 1/2 tsp. rosemary, dried
- 6 tbsp. Swiss cheese, shredded
- 6 tbsp. Romano cheese, shredded
- 6 tbsp. cream cheese
- 1 tsp. soy sauce
- 1 tsp. garlic, minced
- 3 tbsp. green onion, minced

1. Brush the mushroom caps with olive oil; sprinkle with salt, pepper, and rosemary.
2. In a mixing bowl, thoroughly combine the remaining ingredients, mix them well, and divide the filling mixture among the mushroom caps. Cook in the preheated air fryer at 390°F for 7 minutes.
3. Let the mushrooms cool slightly before serving.

PER SERVING

Calories: 344.5 | Fat: 27.5g | Carbs: 10.6g | Protein: 14.8g | Sugars: 7.5g

Cauliflower Balls

Prep time:15 minutes |Cook time: 5 minute |Serves 2

- 1 cup cauliflower, shredded
- 3 oz Mozzarella, shredded
- 1 egg yolk
- 1 tablespoon coconut flour
- ½ teaspoon salt
- ½ teaspoon ground black pepper
- 1 teaspoon cream cheese
- 1 teaspoon sesame oil

1. In the mixing bowl mix up shredded cauliflower, shredded Mozzarella, egg yolk, coconut flour, salt, ground black pepper, and cream cheese.
2. Stir the mixture until it is smooth.
3. with the help of 2 spoons make the balls.
4. Preheat the air fryer to 400F.
5. Put the balls in the air fryer and sprinkle them with sesame oil.
6. Cook the cauliflower rice balls for 5 minutes.

PER SERVING

Calories: 204| Fat: 13.3| Fiber: 2.9| Carbs: 7.1| Protein: 15.3

Cauliflower Pizza Crust

Prep time:10 minutes |Cook time: 6 minutes |Serves 6

- 1 cup cauliflower, shredded
- 1 egg
- ½ cup Cheddar cheese, shredded
- 1 teaspoon salt
- 1 teaspoon keto tomato sauce
- 1 tablespoon coconut flakes
- 1 teaspoon avocado oil

1. Crack the egg in the bowl and whisk it gently.
2. Add shredded cauliflower, cheese, salt, tomato sauce, and coconut flakes.
3. Stir the mixture well.
4. Then put on the baking paper and roll up in the shape of the pizza crust.
5. Sprinkle it with avocado oil.
6. Preheat the air fryer to 400F.
7. Put the baking paper with pizza crust in the air fryer and cook it for 6 minutes.

PER SERVING

Calories: 57| Fat: 4.3| Fiber: 0.5| Carbs: 1.4| Protein: 3.7

Cream Cheese Green Beans

Prep time: 15 minutes | Cook time: 5 minutes | Serves 2

- 8 oz green beans
- 1 egg, beaten
- 1 teaspoon cream cheese
- ¼ cup almond flour
- ¼ cup coconut flakes
- ½ teaspoon ground black pepper
- ½ teaspoon salt
- 1 teaspoon sesame oil

1. In the mixing bowl mix up cream cheese, egg, and ground black pepper.
2. Add salt.
3. In the separated bowl mix up coconut flakes and almond flour.
4. Preheat the air fryer to 400F.
5. Dip the green beans in the egg mixture and then coat in the coconut flakes mixture.
6. Repeat the step one more time and transfer the vegetables in the air fryer.
7. Sprinkle them with sesame oil and cook for 5 minutes.
8. Shake the vegetables after 2 minutes of cooking if you don't put green beans in one layer.

PER SERVING

Calories: 149| Fat: 10.3| Fiber: 5.3| Carbs: 10.9| Protein: 6.1

Feta Peppers

Prep time: 15 minutes | Cook time: 10 minutes | Serves 4

- 5 oz Feta, crumbled
- 8 oz banana pepper, trimmed
- 1 teaspoon sesame oil
- 1 garlic clove, minced
- ½ teaspoon fresh dill, chopped
- 1 teaspoon lemon juice
- ½ teaspoon lime zest, grated

1. Clean the seeds from the peppers and cut them into halves.
2. Then sprinkle the peppers with sesame oil and put in the air fryer.
3. Cook them for 10 minutes at 385F.
4. Flip the peppers on another side after 5 minutes of cooking.
5. Meanwhile, mix up minced garlic, fresh dill, lemon juice, and lime zest.
6. Put the cooked banana peppers on the plate and sprinkle with lemon juice mixture.
7. Then top the vegetables with crumbled feta.

PER SERVING

Calories: 107| Fat: 8.7| Fiber: 0.2| Carbs: 2.2| Protein: 5.2

Herbed Asparagus and Sauce

Prep time: 4 minutes | Cook time: 10 minutes | Serves 4

- 1 pound asparagus, trimmed
- 2 tablespoons olive oil Apinch of salt and black pepper
- 1 teaspoon garlic powder
- 1 teaspoon oregano, dried
- 1 cup Greek yogurt
- 1 cup basil, chopped
- ½ cup parsley, chopped
- ¼ cup chives, chopped
- ¼ cup lemon juice
- 2 garlic cloves, minced

1. In a bowl, mix the asparagus with the oil, salt, pepper, oregano and garlic powder, and toss.
2. Put the asparagus in the air fryer's basket and cook at 400 °F for 10 minutes.
3. Meanwhile, in a blender, mix the yogurt with basil, chives, parsley, lemon juice and garlic cloves and pulse well.
4. Divide the asparagus between plates, drizzle the sauce all over and serve.

PER SERVING

Calories: 194| Fat: 6| Fiber: 2| Carbs: 4| Protein: 8

Mixed Veggies

Prep time: 10 minutes | Cook time: 5 minutes | Serves 4

- ½ cup cauliflower, diced
- ½ cup zucchini, diced
- 1/3 cup cherry tomatoes, chopped
- ¼ cup black olives, chopped
- 3 oz halloumi cheese, chopped
- 1 tablespoon olive oil
- ½ teaspoon chili flakes
- ½ teaspoon dried basil
- ½ teaspoon salt
- Cooking spray

1. Put the diced cauliflower in the air fryer pan.
2. Spray them with cooking spray and then add zucchini.
3. Preheat the air fryer to 395F and put the pan with vegetables inside it.
4. Cook the vegetables for 5 minutes.
5. Then shake them well and transfer in the salad bowl.
6. Add cherry tomatoes, black olives, chopped halloumi, chili flakes, basil, and salt.
7. Then add olive oil and mix up the antipasta.

PER SERVING

Calories: 125| Fat: 25.8| Fiber: 0.9| Carbs: 2.8| Protein: 5.2

Chapter 8

Desserts

Chia and Hemp Pudding

Prep time: 4 hours | Cook time: 2 minutes | Serves 2

- 1 teaspoon hemp seeds
- 1 teaspoon chia seeds
- 1 tablespoon almond flour
- 1 teaspoon coconut flakes
- 1 teaspoon walnuts, chopped
- ½ teaspoon flax meal
- ¼ teaspoon vanilla extract
- ½ teaspoon Erythritol
- ½ cup of coconut milk
- ¼ cup water, boiled

1. Put hemp seeds, chia seeds, almond flour, coconut flakes, walnuts, flax meal, vanilla extract, coconut milk, and water in the big bowl.
2. Stir the mixture until homogenous and pour it into 2 mason jars.
3. Leave the mason jars in the cold place for 4 hours.
4. Then top the surface of the pudding with Erythritol.
5. Place the mason jars in the air fryer and cook the pudding for 2 minutes at 400F or until you get the light brown crust.

PER SERVING

Calories: 257| Fat: 24.2| Fiber: 4.4| Carbs: 8.4| Protein: 5.8

Artichokes and Cream Cheese Dip

Prep time: 5 minutes | Cook time: 25 minutes | Serves 6

- 2 teaspoons olive oil
- 2 spring onions, minced
- 1 pound artichoke hearts, steamed and chopped
- 2 garlic cloves, minced
- 6 ounces cream cheese, soft
- ½ cup almond milk
- 1 cup mozzarella, shredded Apinch of salt and black pepper

1. Grease a baking pan that fits the air fryer with the oil and mix all the ingredients except the mozzarella inside.
2. Sprinkle the cheese all over, introduce the pan in the air fryer and cook at 370 °F for 25 minutes.
3. Divide into bowls and serve as a party dip.

PER SERVING

Calories: 231| Fat: 11| Fiber: 2| Carbs: 4| Protein: 8

Creamy Cheddar Eggs

Prep time: 10 minutes | Cook time: 16 minutes | Serves 8

- 4 eggs
- 2 oz pork rinds
- ¼ cup Cheddar cheese, shredded
- 1 tablespoon heavy cream
- 1 teaspoon fresh dill, chopped

1. Place the eggs in the air fryer and cook them at 255F for 16 minutes.
2. Then cool the eggs in the cold water and peel.
3. Cut every egg into the halves and remove the egg yolks.
4. Transfer the egg yolks in the mixing bowl.
5. Add shredded cheese, heavy cream, and fresh dill.
6. Stir the mixture with the help of the fork until smooth and add pork rinds.
7. Mix it up.
8. Fill the egg whites with the egg yolk mixture.

PER SERVING

Calories: 93| Fat: 6.6| Fiber: 0| Carbs: 0.3| Protein: 8.3

Baked Apple

Prep time: 10 minutes | Cook time: 10 minutes | Serves 4

- 1/4 C. water
- 1/4 tsp. nutmeg
- 1/4 tsp. cinnamon
- 1 1/2 tsp. melted ghee
- 2 tbsp. raisins
- 2 tbsp. chopped walnuts
- 1 medium apple

1. Preheat your air fryer to 350 degrees.
2. Slice an apple in half and discard some of the flesh from the center.
3. Place into a frying pan.
4. Pour water overfilled apples.
5. Place pan with apple halves into the air fryer, bake 20 minutes.

PER SERVING

Calories: 199 | Fat: 9g | Carbs: 17g | Protein: 1g

Date & Hazelnut Cookies

Prep time: 10 minutes | Cook time: 20 minutes | Serves 10

- 3 tablespoons sugar-free maple syrup
- 1/3 cup dated, dried
- ¼ cup hazelnuts, chopped
- 1 stick butter, room temperature
- ½ cup almond flour
- 1/3 teaspoon ground cinnamon
- ½ teaspoon cardamom

1. Firstly, cream the butter with Truvia and maple syrup until mixture is fluffy. Sift both types of flour into bowl with butter mixture. Add remaining ingredients. Now, knead the mixture to form a dough; place in the fridge for 20-minutes.
2. To finish, shape the chilled dough into bite-size balls; arrange them on a baking dish and flatten balls with back of spoon. Bake the cookies for 20-minutes at 310°F.

PER SERVING

Calories: 187 | Total Fat: 10.5g | Carbs: 23.2g | Protein: 1.5g

Cheddar Biscuits

Prep time: 15 minutes | Cook time: 8 minutes | Serves 4

- ½ cup coconut flour
- ¼ cup Cheddar cheese, shredded
- 1 egg, beaten
- 1 tablespoon cream cheese
- 1 tablespoon coconut oil, melted
- ¾ teaspoon baking powder
- ½ teaspoon ground cardamom

1. Mix all ingredients in the mixing bowl and knead the dough.
2. Then make 4 biscuits and put them in the air fryer.
3. Cook the meal at 390F for 8 minutes. Shake the biscuits from time to time to avoid burning.

PER SERVING

Calories: 144 | Fat: 9.2g | Fiber: 6.1g | Carbs: 10.9g | Protein: 5.4 g

The Low-Carb Air Fryer Cookbook

Lemon Olives Dip

Prep time: 5 minutes | Cook time: 5 minutes | Serves 6

- 1 cup black olives, pitted and chopped
- ¼ cup capers
- ½ cup olive oil
- 3 tablespoons lemon juice
- 2 garlic cloves, minced
- 2 teaspoon apple cider vinegar
- 1 cup parsley leaves
- 1 cup basil leaves Apinch of salt and black pepper

1. In a blender, combine all the ingredients, pulse well and transfer to a ramekin.
2. Place the ramekin in your air fryer's basket and cook at 350 °F for 5 minutes.
3. Serve as a snack.

PER SERVING

Calories: 120| Fat: 5| Fiber: 2| Carbs: 3| Protein: 7

Mint Cake

Prep time: 15 minutes | Cook time: 9 minutes | Serves 2

- 1 tablespoon cocoa powder
- 2 tablespoons coconut oil, softened
- 2 tablespoons Erythritol
- 1 teaspoon peppermint
- 3 eggs, beaten
- 1 teaspoon spearmint, dried
- 4 teaspoons almond flour
- Cooking spray

1. Preheat the air fryer to 375°F.
2. Melt the coconut oil in the microwave oven for 10 seconds.
3. Then add cocoa powder and almond flour in the melted coconut oil.
4. After this, add Erythritol, peppermint, and spearmint.
5. Add eggs and whisk the mixture until smooth.
6. Spray the ramekins with cooking spray and pour the chocolate mixture inside.
7. Then put the ramekins with lava cakes in the preheated air fryer and cook them for 9 minutes.
8. Then remove the cooked lava cakes from the air fryer and let them rest for 5 minutes before serving.

PER SERVING

Calories: 538| Fat: 48.5| Fiber: 6.9| Carbs: 14.1| Protein: 20.8

Lemon Pie

Prep time: 10 minutes | Cook time: 35 minutes | Serves 8

- 2 eggs, whisked
- ¾ cup swerve
- ¼ cup coconut flour
- 2 tablespoons butter, melted
- 1 teaspoon lemon zest, grated
- 1 teaspoon baking powder
- 1 teaspoon vanilla extract
- ½ teaspoon lemon extract
- 4 ounces coconut, shredded Cooking spray

1. In a bowl, combine all the ingredients except the cooking spray and stir well.
2. Grease a pie pan that fits the air fryer with the cooking spray, pour the mixture inside, put the pan in the air fryer and cook at 360 °F for 35 minutes.
3. Slice and serve warm.

PER SERVING

Calories: 212| Fat: 15| Fiber: 2| Carbs: 6| Protein: 4

Toffee Apple Upside-Down Breakfast Cake

Prep time: 10 minutes | Cook time: 30 minutes | Serves 9

- ½ cup walnuts, chopped
- 1 lemon, zest
- 1 teaspoon vinegar
- ¾ cup water
- 1 ½ teaspoons mixed spice
- ¼ cup sunflower oil
- 1 teaspoon baking soda
- 1 cup almond flour
- 3 baking apples, cored and sliced
- 2 tablespoon liquid stevia, divided
- ¼ cup almond butter

1. Preheat your air fryer to 390°F. Melt the butter in skillet, then remove from heat and add one tablespoon Stevia and stir. Pour the mixture into baking dish that will fit into your air fryer. Arrange the slices of apples on top and set aside.
2. Combine flour, baking soda, and mixed spice in a large mixing bowl. In another bowl add water, vinegar, remaining tablespoon of liquid Stevia, lemon zest and oil, mix well. Stir in the wet ingredients with dry ingredients and stir until well combined. Pour over apple slices and bake for 30-minutes.

PER SERVING
Calories: 252 | Total Fat: 11.3g | Carbs: 10.2g | Protein: 12.2g

Crustless Cheesecake

Prep time: 5 minutes | Cook time: 10 minutes | Serves 2

- 16 ounces cream cheese, reduced fat, softened
- 2 tablespoons sour cream, reduced fat
- 3/4 cup erythritol sweetener
- 1 teaspoon vanilla extract, unsweetened
- 2 eggs, pastured
- 1/2 teaspoon lemon juice

1. Switch on the air fryer, insert fryer basket, grease it with olive oil, then shut with its lid, set the fryer at 350 °F, and preheat for 5 minutes.
2. Meanwhile, take two 4 inches of springform pans, grease them with oil, and set them aside.
3. Crack the eggs in a bowl and then whisk in lemon juice, sweetener, and vanilla until smooth.
4. Whisk in cream cheese and sour cream until blended, divide the mixture evenly between prepared pans.
5. Open the fryer, place pans in it, close with its lid, and cook for 10 minutes until cakes are set and inserted skewer into the cakes slide out clean.
6. When air fryer beeps, open its lid, take out the cake pans and let cakes cool in them.
7. Take out the cakes, refrigerate for 3 hours until cooled, and then serve.

PER SERVING
Calories: 318 | Fat: 29.7g | Carbs: 1g | Protein: 11.7g

Turmeric Chicken Cubes

Prep time:10 minutes |Cook time: 12 minutes |Serves 6

- 8 oz chicken fillet
- ½ teaspoon ground black pepper
- ½ teaspoon ground turmeric
- ¼ teaspoon ground coriander
- ½ teaspoon ground paprika
- 3 egg whites, whisked
- 4 tablespoons almond flour
- Cooking spray

1. In the shallow bowl mix up ground black pepper, turmeric, coriander, and paprika.
2. Then chop the chicken fillet on the small cubes and sprinkle them with spice mixture.
3. Stir well and ad egg white.
4. Mix up the chicken and egg whites well.
5. After this, coat every chicken cube in the almond flour.
6. Preheat the air fryer to 375°F.
7. Put the chicken cubes in the air fryer basket in one layer and gently spray with cooking spray.
8. Cook the chicken popcorn for 7 minutes.
9. Then shake the chicken popcorn well and cook it for 5 minutes more.

PER SERVING

Calories: 189| Fat: 12.2| Fiber: 2.2| Carbs: 4.5| Protein: 16.8

Cheese Pies

Prep time:15 minutes |Cook time: 4 minutes |Serves 4

- 8 wonton wraps
- 1 egg, beaten
- 1 cup cottage cheese
- 1 tablespoon Erythritol
- ½ teaspoon vanilla extract
- 1 egg white, whisked
- Cooking spray

1. Mix up cottage cheese and Erythritol.
2. Then add vanilla extract and egg.
3. Stir the mixture well with the help of the fork.
4. After this, put the cottage cheese mixture on the wonton wraps and fold them in the shape of pies.
5. Then brush the pies with whisked egg white.
6. Preheat the air fryer to 375°F.
7. Then put the cottage cheese pies in the air fryer and spray them with the cooking spray.
8. Cook the meal for 2 minutes from each side.

PER SERVING

Calories: 92| Fat: 2.2| Fiber: 0| Carbs: 6.3| Protein: 11

The Low-Carb Air Fryer Cookbook

Coconut Cheese Sticks

Prep time: 10 minutes | **Cook time:** 4 minutes | **Serves** 4

- 1 egg, beaten
- 4 tablespoons coconut flakes
- 1 teaspoon ground paprika
- 6 oz Provolone cheese
- Cooking spray

1. Cut the cheese into sticks.
2. Then dip every cheese stick in the beaten egg.
3. After this, mix up coconut flakes and ground paprika.
4. Coat the cheese sticks in the coconut mixture.
5. Preheat the air fryer to 400F.
6. Put the cheese sticks in the air fryer and spray them with cooking spray.
7. Cook the meal for 2 minutes from each side.
8. Cool them well before serving.

PER SERVING

Calories: 184| Fat: 14.2| Fiber: 0.7| Carbs: 2.1| Protein: 12.5

Olives Fritters

Prep time: 5 minutes | **Cook time:** 12 minutes | **Serves** 6

- Cooking spray
- ½ cup parsley, chopped
- 1 egg
- ½ cup almond flour
- Salt and black pepper to the taste
- 3 spring onions, chopped
- ½ cup kalamata olives, pitted and minced
- 3 zucchinis, grated

1. In a bowl, mix all the ingredients except the cooking spray, stir well and shape medium fritters out of this mixture.
2. Place the fritters in your air fryer's basket, grease them with cooking spray and cook at 380 °F for 6 minutes on each side.
3. Serve them as an appetizer.

PER SERVING

Calories: 165| Fat: 5| Fiber: 2| Carbs: 3| Protein: 7

Herbed Cheese Balls

Prep time: 20 minutes | **Cook time:** 9 minutes | **Serves** 3

- 1 teaspoon garlic powder
- 1 oz Parmesan, grated
- ½ cup Cheddar cheese, shredded
- 1 egg, beaten
- 1 tablespoon cream cheese
- 1 teaspoon dried dill
- 1 teaspoon dried cilantro
- 1 teaspoon dried parsley
- Cooking spray

1. Mix up Parmesan and Cheddar cheese.
2. Add garlic powder, egg, cream cheese, dried dill, cilantro, and parsley.
3. Stir the mixture until homogenous.
4. with the help of the scoop make the cheese balls and put them in the freezer for 15 minutes.
5. Preheat the air fryer to 400F.
6. Then spray the air fryer basket with cooking spray.
7. Put the frozen cheese balls in the air fryer basket.
8. Cook them for 9 minutes or until they are golden brown.

PER SERVING

Calories: 143| Fat: 10.9| Fiber: 0.1| Carbs: 1.7| Protein: 10.1

Appendix 1 Measurement Conversion Chart

Volume Equivalents (Dry)	
US STANDARD	METRIC (APPROXIMATE)
1/8 teaspoon	0.5 mL
1/4 teaspoon	1 mL
1/2 teaspoon	2 mL
3/4 teaspoon	4 mL
1 teaspoon	5 mL
1 tablespoon	15 mL
1/4 cup	59 mL
1/2 cup	118 mL
3/4 cup	177 mL
1 cup	235 mL
2 cups	475 mL
3 cups	700 mL
4 cups	1 L

Volume Equivalents (Liquid)		
US STANDARD	US STANDARD (OUNCES)	METRIC (APPROXIMATE)
2 tablespoons	1 fl.oz.	30 mL
1/4 cup	2 fl.oz.	60 mL
1/2 cup	4 fl.oz.	120 mL
1 cup	8 fl.oz.	240 mL
1 1/2 cup	12 fl.oz.	355 mL
2 cups or 1 pint	16 fl.oz.	475 mL
4 cups or 1 quart	32 fl.oz.	1 L
1 gallon	128 fl.oz.	4 L

Temperatures Equivalents	
FAHRENHEIT(F)	CELSIUS(C) APPROXIMATE)
225 °F	107 °C
250 °F	120 ° °C
275 °F	135 °C
300 °F	150 °C
325 °F	160 °C
350 °F	180 °C
375 °F	190 °C
400 °F	205 °C
425 °F	220 °C
450 °F	235 °C
475 °F	245 °C
500 °F	260 °C

Weight Equivalents	
US STANDARD	METRIC (APPROXIMATE)
1 ounce	28 g
2 ounces	57 g
5 ounces	142 g
10 ounces	284 g
15 ounces	425 g
16 ounces (1 pound)	455 g
1.5 pounds	680 g
2 pounds	907 g

Appendix 2 The Dirty Dozen and Clean Fifteen

The Environmental Working Group (EWG) is a nonprofit, nonpartisan organization dedicated to protecting human health and the environment Its mission is to empower people to live healthier lives in a healthier environment. This organization publishes an annual list of the twelve kinds of produce, in sequence, that have the highest amount of pesticide residue-the Dirty Dozen-as well as a list of the fifteen kinds ofproduce that have the least amount of pesticide residue-the Clean Fifteen.

THE DIRTY DOZEN

The 2016 Dirty Dozen includes the following produce. These are considered among the year's most important produce to buy organic:

Strawberries	Spinach
Apples	Tomatoes
Nectarines	Bell peppers
Peaches	Cherry tomatoes
Celery	Cucumbers
Grapes	Kale/collard greens
Cherries	Hot peppers

The Dirty Dozen list contains two additional itemskale/collard greens and hot peppers-because they tend to contain trace levels of highly hazardous pesticides.

THE CLEAN FIFTEEN

The least critical to buy organically are the Clean Fifteen list. The following are on the 2016 list:

Avocados	Papayas
Corn	Kiw
Pineapples	Eggplant
Cabbage	Honeydew
Sweet peas	Grapefruit
Onions	Cantaloupe
Asparagus	Cauliflower
Mangos	

Some of the sweet corn sold in the United States are made from genetically engineered (GE) seedstock. Buy organic varieties of these crops to avoid GE produce.

Appendix 3 Index

A

almond flour 11, 14, 17, 19, 20, 21, 22, 23, 24, 25, 48, 57, 58, 60, 66
apple 17, 18, 28, 40, 51, 52, 61, 63, 67, 74, 75
apple cider vinegar 17, 18, 28, 40, 51, 52, 61
asparagus 32, 33, 34, 67, 71
avocado 9, 19, 21, 24, 27, 28, 29, 31, 32, 36

B

bacon 8, 25, 27, 39, 40, 59, 63
basil 9, 18, 22, 25, 30, 31, 40, 53, 57, 59, 60, 63, 68, 71
bell pepper 9, 18, 37, 47, 48, 51, 63
bread 11, 12, 21, 22, 57, 59
broccoli 13, 17, 27, 60, 61
buns 9, 14, 48
butter 8, 12, 14, 15, 20, 21, 22, 23, 24, 25, 30, 31

C

cauliflower 9, 20, 36, 42, 52, 55, 56, 58, 61
cayenne 8, 30, 45, 52
Cheddar cheese 22, 25, 37, 41, 55, 56, 69, 73, 74
cheese 8, 11, 12, 13, 17, 19, 22, 23, 24
chicken 18, 20, 22, 23, 25, 27, 28, 29, 30, 31
chili powder 11, 20, 29, 30, 39, 42, 47, 50, 51, 61
chives 8, 40, 44, 45, 53, 57, 58, 71

cinnamon 8, 17, 19, 74
coconut 8, 13, 17, 20, 21, 22, 24, 25
coriander 11, 24, 40, 42, 50, 64, 77
cumin 11, 19, 27, 43, 61

D

Dijon mustard 48
dried cilantro 18, 19, 33, 41, 42, 57, 58, 78
dried dill 22, 23, 36, 38, 39, 78
dried parsley 22, 34, 36, 47, 56, 66, 78

E

egg 8, 10, 11, 13, 14, 17, 18, 19, 20, 21, 22, 23
Erythritol 8, 17, 19, 25, 32, 73, 75

F

fillet 20, 21, 27, 29, 30, 50, 52, 57, 67, 77
fish 21, 50, 51, 52, 53, 57
flax meal 49, 73
fresh dill 70, 73

G

garlic 9, 10, 11, 12, 13, 14, 19, 20, 22, 27
garlic powder 11, 13, 14, 20, 22, 29, 32, 37, 38
Greek yogurt 21, 71

H

hazelnuts 74

hemp seeds 73

I

Italian seasoning 22, 49

J

juice 24, 33, 34, 39, 40, 43, 47, 50, 51, 53, 66, 70

K

kalamata olives 40, 78
kale 22, 59
ketchup 64
kosher salt 31, 49, 51, 66

L

lemon juice 24, 33, 34, 40, 43, 47, 51, 53, 66, 70
lime juice 39, 50
liquid stevia 12, 76

M

maple syrup 74
marinara sauce 41
mayonnaise 9, 14, 48, 64
melted ghee 23, 74
milk 12, 17, 39, 60, 61, 73
Mozzarella 13, 21, 22, 23, 24, 25, 55, 57, 59
mustard 24, 37, 44, 48, 59, 64, 67

N

nutritional yeast 11, 57

O

olive oil 9, 10, 13, 14, 15, 19, 23, 27

onion 9, 10, 11, 12, 14, 18, 19, 20, 21, 24, 27, 30
oregano 8, 18, 21, 22, 23, 29, 30, 31, 33, 34, 41, 53, 57, 71

P

paprika 8, 13, 23, 27, 28, 32, 33, 34, 43, 50, 52, 66, 67, 77, 78
Parmesan 13, 30, 49, 55, 57, 78
peppermint 75
potato 9, 59, 61, 66
Provolone cheese 22, 29, 42, 78

R

raisins 74

S

salt 8, 9, 11, 12, 13, 14, 15, 17, 18, 19, 20, 21
soy sauce 10, 12, 15, 38, 51, 69

T

tomato 9, 14, 18, 19, 25, 27, 32, 34, 36, 37, 38, 41
turmeric 18, 28, 36, 45, 52, 58, 59, 60

W

walnuts 73, 74, 76
white cabbage 24, 38, 42, 67

Y

yogurt 8, 21, 71

Z

zucchini 9, 11, 15, 36, 44, 71

Hey there!

Wow, can you believe we've reached the end of this culinary journey together? I'm truly thrilled and filled with joy as I think back on all the recipes we've shared and the flavors we've discovered. This experience, blending a bit of tradition with our own unique twists, has been a journey of love for good food. And knowing you've been out there, giving these dishes a try, has made this adventure incredibly special to me.

Even though we're turning the last page of this book, I hope our conversation about all things delicious doesn't have to end. I cherish your thoughts, your experiments, and yes, even those moments when things didn't go as planned. Every piece of feedback you share is invaluable, helping to enrich this experience for us all.

I'd be so grateful if you could take a moment to share your thoughts with me, be it through a review on Amazon or any other place you feel comfortable expressing yourself online. Whether it's praise, constructive criticism, or even an idea for how we might do things differently in the future, your input is what truly makes this journey meaningful.

This book is a piece of my heart, offered to you with all the love and enthusiasm I have for cooking. But it's your engagement and your words that elevate it to something truly extraordinary.

Thank you from the bottom of my heart for being such an integral part of this culinary adventure. Your openness to trying new things and sharing your experiences has been the greatest gift.

Catch you later,

Christina J. Williamson